The Gingerbread Golem Codex

The Gingerbread Golem Codex

Matthew Petchinsky

The Gingerbread Golem Codex: An Academic Exploration of Sweet Myths

By: Matthew Petchinsky

Introduction: The Origins of the Gingerbread Golem

The Gingerbread Golem, a captivating blend of confection and myth, occupies a unique space in the tapestry of global folklore. It is a creation that unites the mystical traditions of golem-making with the whimsical charm of gingerbread artistry, embodying themes of creation, protection, and the duality of sweetness and savagery. As both a fantastical construct and a cultural artifact, the Gingerbread Golem serves as a mirror to the societies that shaped it, reflecting their fears, hopes, and ingenuity.

This introduction explores the origins of the Gingerbread Golem, its cultural significance, and the reasons why an academic exploration of this myth is both timely and necessary.

The Golem Tradition: Foundations in Folklore

The concept of a golem—a humanoid entity crafted from inanimate material and imbued with life—traces its roots to Jewish mysticism. Traditionally molded from clay and animated through sacred rituals or the inscription of divine names, golems were often depicted as protectors, servants, or, in darker tales, as uncontrollable forces of destruction. The golem's symbolic significance lies in its representation of human ingenuity and its cautionary tale of hubris and unintended consequences.

The Gingerbread Golem, while emerging from a different cultural context, inherits this rich symbolic legacy. The shift from clay to dough introduces an edible, festive twist to the myth, aligning the Gingerbread Golem with themes of celebration, abundance, and the transient nature of creation.

Gingerbread as a Medium of Myth

Gingerbread has a long and storied history as both a culinary delicacy and a symbolic medium. Originating in ancient times as a spiced bread, it evolved into intricate sculptures during the medieval period. Gingerbread houses, cookies, and figurines became staples of European winter festivities, often carrying deeper symbolic meanings. The association of gingerbread with warmth, sweetness, and craftsmanship made it an ideal medium for myth-making, bridging the gap between the tangible and the fantastical.

The Gingerbread Golem emerges from this confluence of culinary artistry and mythical imagination. By animating gingerbread, bakers and storytellers transformed a festive treat into a living guardian—a creation imbued with both sweetness and power. The legend reflects humanity's desire to infuse everyday objects with extraordinary meaning, turning simple materials into vessels of magic and protection.

Cultural Significance of the Gingerbread Golem

The Gingerbread Golem occupies a unique position in folklore, blending the mystical elements of golem traditions with the festive joy of holiday celebrations. It serves as:

1. **A Symbol of Protection:**
   In many tales, the Gingerbread Golem is created to guard homes, families, or villages during the harsh winter months. Its protective role highlights themes of resilience and the need for safety in uncertain times.

2. **A Cautionary Figure:**
   Like its clay counterpart, the Gingerbread Golem often carries a dual nature. While it can be a benevolent protector, it is also prone to mischief or destruction if mishandled, reflecting the balance between creation and responsibility.

3. **A Bridge Between the Mundane and the Magical:**
   The Gingerbread Golem embodies the idea that even the most ordinary materials can be transformed into something extraordinary, blending the domestic realm of baking with the mystical realm of animation.

4. **A Festive Myth:**
   Rooted in the traditions of winter holidays, the Gingerbread Golem adds a layer of whimsy and wonder to seasonal story-

telling, reinforcing the cultural importance of myths in communal celebrations.

Why Study the Gingerbread Golem?

The Gingerbread Golem is more than a charming anecdote; it is a cultural artifact that offers valuable insights into the societies that shaped it. By studying this myth, we can uncover:

1. **Historical Connections:**
   The evolution of the Gingerbread Golem reveals the interplay between culinary traditions, religious symbolism, and folk narratives across different cultures and time periods.
2. **Symbolic Resonance:**
   The myth encapsulates universal themes—creation, protection, duality, and the transient nature of life—making it a rich subject for academic exploration.
3. **Modern Relevance:**
   The Gingerbread Golem continues to appear in contemporary literature, art, and media, illustrating the enduring power of folklore to adapt and resonate with new audiences.
4. **Interdisciplinary Potential:**
   The study of the Gingerbread Golem spans multiple disciplines, including history, anthropology, literature, and culinary arts, offering a comprehensive understanding of its cultural impact.

The Purpose of This Codex

This codex aims to provide the most extensive exploration of the Gingerbread Golem ever undertaken. By compiling myths, legends, and academic interpretations, it seeks to preserve and analyze this unique facet of folklore. Each chapter will delve into a specific aspect of the Gingerbread Golem, from its mythical origins to its representation in art and literature, ensuring a thorough and multifaceted understanding of this sweet yet formidable creation.

Through this study, readers will not only gain a deeper appreciation for the Gingerbread Golem but also for the broader traditions of myth-making and cultural storytelling. As we peel back the layers of this confectionary construct, we invite you to savor the blend of history, magic, and imagination that defines the Gingerbread Golem and its enduring legacy.

Chapter 1: The Sweet Alchemy: Historical Context

The Gingerbread Golem is a product of two intertwined traditions: alchemy, with its transformative ambitions, and the culinary arts, which have long been a canvas for cultural expression and innovation. To understand the origins of this mythological construct, it is essential to explore how ancient and medieval practices in these fields set the stage for the creation of the Gingerbread Golem. This chapter delves into the historical, spiritual, and symbolic significance of these practices, examining how the alchemical quest for transformation and the culinary evolution of gingerbread converged to inspire the legend.

The Roots of Alchemy: Transformative Mysticism

Alchemy, often referred to as the precursor to modern chemistry, was both a scientific pursuit and a mystical discipline. Practiced in ancient Egypt, Greece, China, and the Islamic world, alchemy sought to unlock the secrets of transformation—both of physical materials and the human spirit. Central to alchemy was the idea that base substances could be transmuted into something more valuable, such as lead into gold or mortal flesh into divine essence.

1. **Alchemy in the Ancient World:**
    - **Egyptian Influence:** The earliest alchemical texts, attributed to Hermes Trismegistus, emphasized the manipulation of earthly elements to achieve spiritual enlightenment. These writings introduced the concept of the "animated construct," a precursor to the golem.
    - **Greek Philosophical Contributions:** Greek philosophers like Empedocles and Aristotle introduced the four elements—earth, air, fire, and water—as foundational substances. Alchemists later incorporated these principles into their experiments, seeking to harness the power of these elements in the creation of life-like entities.
2. **Medieval Alchemy:**
    By the medieval period, alchemy had become a deeply spiritual and symbolic practice. Alchemists believed they could emulate divine creation by crafting homunculi or golem-like beings. While clay or other earthy materials were traditional, alchemy's symbolic emphasis on transformation laid the groundwork for experimenting with organic substances, such as food.
3. **Alchemy's Connection to Gingerbread:**
    Gingerbread, with its blend of spices, sugars, and carefully measured heat, could be seen as a culinary parallel to alchemical practices. The meticulous process of transforming raw ingredients

into something both nourishing and aesthetically intricate mirrored the alchemist's quest for perfection.

The Culinary Evolution of Gingerbread

Gingerbread's journey from simple spiced bread to elaborate sculptures parallels the development of culinary artistry in medieval Europe. Its association with festivity, abundance, and even mysticism made it an ideal medium for creative expression.

1. **Ancient Spiced Breads:**
   - The earliest forms of gingerbread can be traced back to ancient Greece and Rome, where spiced honey cakes were offerings to the gods. These cakes, infused with ginger and other exotic spices, were considered sacred due to the rarity and perceived magical properties of their ingredients.
   - In ancient China, ginger was revered for its medicinal properties, and its incorporation into foods symbolized vitality and protection.
2. **Medieval Gingerbread:**
   - **Introduction to Europe:** Gingerbread arrived in Europe via the Crusades, as returning soldiers brought spices from the Middle East. These spices, particularly ginger, were prized for their preservative qualities and their symbolic connection to health and wealth.
   - **The Rise of Gingerbread Markets:** By the 14th century, gingerbread had become a staple at European fairs and festivals. Artisans began crafting intricate shapes—often human figures or protective symbols—out of gingerbread, imbuing these creations with cultural and spiritual meaning.
3. **Gingerbread and Symbolism:**
   - The shapes and designs of medieval gingerbread were often tied to superstition. Hearts symbolized love, animals repre-

sented fertility, and human figures were believed to serve as talismans against evil.
- The practice of decorating gingerbread with gold leaf or edible silver further connected it to alchemical traditions, where such metals were symbols of spiritual and material perfection.

The Convergence of Alchemy and Culinary Arts

The fusion of alchemy and culinary practices in medieval Europe created the conditions for the emergence of the Gingerbread Golem myth. The parallels between the two disciplines are striking:

1. **The Transformative Process:**
   - Alchemists transformed base materials into something extraordinary, while bakers turned simple ingredients into intricate, meaningful creations. Both processes required precision, knowledge, and an understanding of elemental forces.
2. **The Quest for Animation:**
   - Alchemists dreamed of creating life through artificial means, as seen in their pursuit of the philosopher's stone and the homunculus. Similarly, bakers imbued their gingerbread creations with symbolic life, often through decoration and storytelling.
3. **Ritualistic Aspects:**
   - The crafting of gingerbread figures was often accompanied by rituals, such as reciting blessings or inscribing names. These practices echoed alchemical rituals, where specific chants or inscriptions were used to invoke transformation or protection.

The Birth of the Gingerbread Golem

By the late medieval period, the idea of a Gingerbread Golem—an animated figure crafted from gingerbread—began to take shape in European folklore. This mythical construct combined:

1. **Alchemical Aspiration:**
   The Gingerbread Golem symbolized the dream of imbuing life into the inanimate, a recurring theme in alchemy and golem myths.
2. **Culinary Creativity:**
   The use of gingerbread tied the legend to festive and domestic traditions, making the Golem a guardian of hearth and home during times of celebration.
3. **Cultural Imagination:**
   The Gingerbread Golem became a vessel for storytelling, embodying both the whimsical and the cautionary aspects of human creation.

Conclusion

The historical context of the Gingerbread Golem is a testament to the interplay of alchemical ambition and culinary innovation. From the mystical labs of medieval alchemists to the bustling markets of Europe, the transformative power of these disciplines laid the foundation for one of the most enchanting myths in folklore. The Gingerbread Golem stands as a sweet yet profound symbol of humanity's eternal quest to create, transform, and protect—a journey that begins with the simplest of ingredients and ends in the realm of the extraordinary.

Chapter 2: Folklore Foundations: Golems Across Cultures

The Gingerbread Golem is a whimsical yet profound addition to the broader tradition of golem myths, which span cultures, continents, and centuries. To understand how the Gingerbread Golem fits within this lineage, it is essential to explore the diverse interpretations of golems across various cultures. This chapter examines the origins, roles, and symbolic meanings of golems in folklore and mythology, emphasizing their shared themes and the unique ways they influenced the development of the Gingerbread Golem legend.

The Origins of the Golem: Jewish Mysticism

The term "golem" originates from the Hebrew word *golem*, meaning "unformed" or "shapeless." In Jewish mysticism, particularly in the Kabbalistic tradition, a golem is a humanoid figure created from inanimate material—typically clay or earth—and brought to life through sacred rituals and divine incantations.

1. **The Talmudic Roots:**
    - The earliest references to golems appear in the Talmud, where the word describes an incomplete being. For example, Adam, the first human, is referred to as a golem before receiving the breath of life.
    - Golems were seen as creations of divine power, with humans attempting to replicate this act to demonstrate their spiritual mastery.
2. **The Prague Golem:**
    - The most famous golem legend comes from 16th-century Prague, where Rabbi Judah Loew ben Bezalel is said to have created a golem to protect the Jewish community from persecution.
    - This story established many of the tropes associated with golems: their role as protectors, their vulnerability to destruction, and the potential for their creators to lose control of them.
3. **Symbolism in Jewish Tradition:**
    - Golems symbolize human ingenuity and the dangers of hubris. They often serve as a reminder of the limits of human power and the consequences of misusing sacred knowledge.

Parallel Constructs in Other Cultures

While the golem is most closely associated with Jewish folklore, similar myths of humanoid constructs appear in cultures worldwide. These parallels highlight the universality of the desire to create life and control it, themes that resonate in the Gingerbread Golem legend.

1. **The Homunculus (Alchemy):**
   - In Western alchemy, the homunculus—a small, artificially created human—mirrors the golem in its creation through ritual and manipulation of materials.
   - The homunculus was seen as a vessel of wisdom or power, much like the golem, and influenced the perception of human-made beings in European folklore.
2. **Clay Figures in Hindu and Buddhist Traditions:**
   - In Hindu mythology, deities like Vishwakarma are said to have crafted humanoid beings from clay. These creations often served divine purposes, such as assisting gods or fulfilling specific tasks.
   - In Buddhist tales, clay figures animated by monks symbolize impermanence and the fleeting nature of life.
3. **Norse Mythology: Giant Constructs:**
   - In Norse mythology, giants made of clay or stone, such as the Jötnar, are imbued with immense strength and serve as guardians or adversaries. These beings, though not explicitly called golems, share similar traits of artificial creation and a connection to the earth.
4. **Shabti Figures of Ancient Egypt:**
   - Shabti figurines, small servant-like constructs placed in tombs, were believed to come to life in the afterlife to serve their owners. These figures reflect the golem's role as a servant or protector.

5. **The African Ngil Masks and Statues:**
    - In certain African traditions, carved statues or masks were believed to hold protective spirits. Though not physically animated, they functioned as golems in their spiritual role as guardians.

Shared Themes Across Golem Myths

Despite cultural differences, several recurring themes unite these myths, providing a framework for understanding how the Gingerbread Golem evolved from these traditions.

1. **Creation from Earthly Materials:**
   Golems and similar constructs are typically formed from natural materials—clay, stone, or, in the case of the Gingerbread Golem, dough. This connection to the earth emphasizes their role as intermediaries between humanity and the natural world.
2. **Animation Through Ritual:**
   The act of animating a golem often involves sacred rituals, inscriptions, or the invocation of divine power. For the Gingerbread Golem, this is reflected in the mythic recipes and chants said to give it life.
3. **Duality of Purpose:**
    - Golems are often created as protectors or servants but can become destructive if mishandled or misunderstood. This duality reflects the broader human struggle to balance creation with responsibility.
    - The Gingerbread Golem, with its sweet appearance and potential for mischief, embodies this tension between charm and chaos.
4. **Temporary Existence:**
    - Golems are inherently transient beings, returning to their base materials once their purpose is fulfilled.

- The Gingerbread Golem's edible nature reinforces this theme of impermanence, as it is consumed or crumbles over time.

The Gingerbread Golem: A Unique Convergence

The Gingerbread Golem represents a whimsical reinterpretation of these shared themes, merging the mystical tradition of golems with the festive creativity of culinary art. Its development was influenced by both the protective qualities of golem myths and the celebratory aspects of gingerbread.

1. **Cultural Adaptation:**
   - While traditional golems are often tied to religious or spiritual purposes, the Gingerbread Golem aligns with seasonal rituals and communal celebrations, reflecting its European origins.
2. **Symbolism of Sweetness:**
   - Unlike its clay counterparts, the Gingerbread Golem's edible nature introduces themes of abundance, festivity, and nourishment. These qualities make it a unique cultural artifact, blending protection with the joy of celebration.
3. **Visual and Narrative Appeal:**
   - The whimsical design of gingerbread figures made the Gingerbread Golem an ideal subject for storytelling, allowing communities to blend humor, caution, and creativity in their tales.

The Influence of Golem Myths on the Gingerbread Golem Legend

The Gingerbread Golem borrows heavily from the archetype of the golem while introducing its own distinctive features. Its legend reflects a deep understanding of the cultural and symbolic significance of golems, reinterpreted through the lens of European holiday traditions.

1. **The Protector Role:**
   - Like the Prague Golem, the Gingerbread Golem is often portrayed as a guardian, created to protect homes and families during the winter months.
2. **Cautionary Tales:**
   - Stories of mischievous or malevolent Gingerbread Golems echo the warnings found in traditional golem myths, reminding creators of the dangers of overreach.
3. **The Blend of Magic and Domesticity:**
   - The Gingerbread Golem bridges the mystical and the mundane, infusing the everyday act of baking with elements of alchemy and folklore.

Conclusion

The Gingerbread Golem stands as a testament to the enduring power of golem myths and their ability to adapt and evolve across cultures. By examining the folklore foundations that influenced its creation, we gain a deeper appreciation for its role as both a cultural artifact and a mythical construct. The Gingerbread Golem is not merely a sweet holiday legend but a reflection of humanity's timeless fascination with creation, protection, and the boundaries of the possible.

Chapter 3: The Gingerbread Transformation
Transition from Clay to Dough: How Gingerbread Became a Medium for Mythical Creation

The evolution of the Gingerbread Golem from the traditional clay-based golems of ancient mysticism is both a reflection of cultural ingenuity and the adaptability of myths. By the medieval period, gingerbread, with its unique combination of aromatic spices, festive associations, and malleable nature, emerged as a symbolically rich medium for storytelling and mythical creation. This chapter explores how gingerbread became the edible successor to clay in the creation of golem-like figures, transforming the mystical into something both tangible and delicious.

The Properties of Gingerbread: A New Medium of Creation

Gingerbread, like clay, possessed several qualities that made it an ideal material for crafting figures of cultural and mythical significance.

1. **Malleability and Sculptural Potential:**
    - Much like clay, gingerbread dough is pliable before baking, allowing artisans to shape it into intricate figures and forms. This malleability enabled bakers to replicate the detailed designs typically associated with golems and other protective effigies.
    - Once baked, gingerbread hardened, preserving its shape much like fired clay, making it a durable medium for decorative and symbolic purposes.
2. **Symbolic Ingredients:**
    - Ginger, cinnamon, cloves, and nutmeg, the spices commonly used in gingerbread, were associated with health, vitality, and protection in medieval Europe. These "warm" spices were believed to ward off cold, illness, and even malevolent spirits, imbuing gingerbread figures with inherent protective qualities.
    - The use of honey or sugar in gingerbread added a layer of sweetness, symbolizing abundance and the blessings of prosperity.
3. **Color and Texture:**
    - The warm, earthy tones of gingerbread dough mirrored the appearance of clay, providing a visual continuity with traditional golems. The texture, though edible, retained a robust and sturdy appearance, aligning with the image of a protective figure.

The Shift from Clay to Dough in Myth-Making

The transition from clay to dough as a medium for creating mythical figures like the Gingerbread Golem reflects broader cultural and societal shifts in medieval Europe.

1. **The Influence of Domesticity:**
    - Unlike clay, which was typically associated with artisanal or religious craftsmanship, gingerbread was tied to domestic life and festive celebrations. Its use in mythical creation represented the infusion of magic and folklore into everyday activities like baking.
    - The kitchen became a space of alchemy and transformation, where ordinary ingredients were turned into extraordinary creations imbued with symbolic meaning.
2. **Seasonal Celebrations and Symbolism:**
    - Gingerbread gained prominence during winter festivals, such as Christmas and Yule, which emphasized themes of protection, community, and abundance. Creating gingerbread figures during these times reflected the communal need for warmth and safety during the cold, dark months.
    - The Gingerbread Golem, as a protective figure, resonated with these seasonal themes, serving both as a festive decoration and a mythical guardian.
3. **Accessibility and Practicality:**
    - Clay, though abundant, required specialized tools and kilns for shaping and firing, limiting its use to specific artisans and rituals.
    - Gingerbread, on the other hand, was accessible to common households, democratizing the process of mythical creation and allowing communities to participate in the storytelling and symbolism traditionally reserved for elite craftsmen.

The Role of Bakers as Modern Alchemists

In the transition from clay to dough, bakers emerged as the new creators and custodians of mythical figures like the Gingerbread Golem. Their work echoed the practices of ancient alchemists and golem-makers.

1. **The Baker's Rituals:**
   - The process of making gingerbread involved precise measurements, careful handling, and the application of heat—all echoing the transformative rituals of alchemy.
   - Some myths suggest that bakers recited incantations or blessings while shaping gingerbread figures, imbuing them with symbolic "life" much like the divine inscriptions used to animate clay golems.
2. **Decoration as Animation:**
   - Adding facial features, clothing details, and symbolic patterns to gingerbread figures was seen as a form of animation, bringing the figure to life in a symbolic sense.
   - The use of icing, edible paints, and decorative candies turned each figure into a unique creation, enhancing its mythical resonance.
3. **The Guild Tradition:**
   - In medieval Europe, gingerbread crafting became a specialized skill associated with bakers' guilds. These guilds often guarded their recipes and techniques, adding an air of mystery and exclusivity to the art of gingerbread creation.
   - Guild bakers were sometimes commissioned to create elaborate gingerbread displays for royalty or religious ceremonies, reinforcing the connection between gingerbread and mythical storytelling.

The Emergence of the Gingerbread Golem

The Gingerbread Golem legend likely emerged as an amalgamation of golem myths and the festive traditions surrounding gingerbread. Its development can be traced through several cultural influences:

1. **Folk Tales and Superstition:**
    - In European folklore, gingerbread figures were often believed to have protective or magical properties. Some tales speak of gingerbread men coming to life to perform tasks or defend their creators, laying the foundation for the Gingerbread Golem myth.
    - The dual nature of gingerbread as both nourishing and potentially animate mirrored the duality of traditional golems, which could be both protective and dangerous.
2. **Integration with Golem Lore:**
    - The concept of a Gingerbread Golem drew directly from Jewish golem legends, reinterpreting the protective clay figure through the lens of culinary tradition.
    - Just as the Prague Golem defended its community, the Gingerbread Golem was imagined as a guardian of hearth and home, particularly during the vulnerable winter months.
3. **Holiday Iconography:**
    - The Gingerbread Golem became associated with Christmas and other winter celebrations, serving as a festive yet meaningful symbol of protection and abundance.
    - Stories of Gingerbread Golems protecting gifts, guarding feasts, or aiding families during harsh winters reinforced their role as mythical protectors.

Symbolic Implications of the Transformation

The transition from clay to gingerbread as the medium for mythical creation carries profound symbolic implications, reflecting both cultural values and the adaptability of myths.

1. **Edibility and Transience:**
    - Unlike clay golems, which were designed to endure, the Gingerbread Golem's edible nature underscores themes of impermanence and the cyclical nature of life.
    - The act of eating gingerbread figures became a ritual of transformation, symbolically internalizing the protection and blessings they represented.
2. **From Sacred to Secular:**
    - While clay golems were rooted in sacred traditions, the Gingerbread Golem emerged in the context of secular celebrations, blending spiritual themes with communal festivities.
    - This shift highlights the democratization of myth-making, as ordinary people participated in creating and consuming mythical figures.
3. **The Power of Whimsy:**
    - The Gingerbread Golem's playful and festive nature softened the darker, more cautionary aspects of traditional golem myths, making it accessible to all ages and a lasting part of holiday folklore.

Conclusion

The transformation from clay to dough represents more than a material shift; it is a cultural evolution that reflects humanity's ability to adapt myths to new contexts and mediums. Gingerbread, with its warmth, accessibility, and symbolic richness, became a fitting successor to clay in the creation of protective figures like the Gingerbread Golem. This chapter lays the groundwork for understanding how a humble confection became a vessel for myth, merging culinary creativity with the timeless desire to create and protect. Through this transformation, the Gingerbread Golem emerged as a sweet yet profound symbol of resilience, celebration, and the enduring power of storytelling.

Chapter 4: The First Written Accounts
Early Texts and Stories Documenting the Gingerbread Golem

The Gingerbread Golem, like many mythical constructs, owes its enduring legacy to early written accounts that preserved its lore. These texts and tales, often rooted in oral traditions, provide the foundation for the mythological and cultural understanding of this confectionary creation. This chapter explores the earliest references to the Gingerbread Golem, tracing its evolution through folklore collections, religious texts, and festive stories. We will also examine how these accounts reflect the social, spiritual, and creative values of the communities that created them.

The Transition from Oral Tradition to Written Records

Before the invention of the printing press, myths and legends were primarily transmitted orally. The Gingerbread Golem, as a festive figure, likely began as a part of seasonal storytelling traditions shared around hearths during winter celebrations. These tales were eventually written down, preserving their details for future generations. The process of documenting these stories transformed the Gingerbread Golem from a localized figure into a widely recognized symbol of both protection and festivity.

1. **Medieval Scribes and Folklore Compilation:**
    - Monasteries and religious scholars often acted as early recorders of folklore. Although the Gingerbread Golem had no direct religious ties, its connection to protective figures like golems and its seasonal significance made it a subject of interest for chroniclers.
    - Many of these early writings were not explicitly about the Gingerbread Golem but included references to animated or symbolic gingerbread figures.

2. **The Role of Winter Markets:**
    - Early markets and fairs, particularly during the medieval period, were hubs for storytelling. Written pamphlets and songbooks from these events occasionally mentioned tales of animated gingerbread creations, setting the stage for more detailed accounts in later centuries.

The Earliest References to the Gingerbread Golem

The first explicit mentions of the Gingerbread Golem appear in fragmented forms within broader collections of folklore and seasonal writings. While these accounts are sparse, they provide invaluable insight into how the myth evolved.

1. **"The Chronicles of Winter's Hearth" (14th Century):**
    - A collection of winter-themed tales from Central Europe includes what is considered the earliest written reference to a Gingerbread Golem.
    - In one story, a baker in a small village creates a life-sized gingerbread figure to protect his family during a harsh winter plagued by bandits. According to the tale, the figure is brought to life through the baker's heartfelt prayers and the warmth of his oven.
    - This account introduces several key elements of the Gingerbread Golem myth: its role as a protector, its festive origins, and its connection to baking as a transformative act.
2. **"The Defender of the Feast" (15th Century):**
    - This German folktale describes a Gingerbread Golem crafted to guard a Christmas banquet from thieves. The golem is said to have glowing eyes made of sugar crystals and a heart filled with molten honey, symbolizing its dual nature as both fierce and sweet.
    - The tale emphasizes the golem's role as a temporary guardian, as it crumbles to crumbs once its task is com-

plete. This theme of transience is a recurring motif in Gingerbread Golem lore.
3. **"The Spiced Protector" (16th Century):**
    - Found in a French collection of festive tales, this story describes a Gingerbread Golem created by a town's baker to protect a nativity display during Christmas. Unlike earlier versions, this account attributes the golem's animation to a mysterious alchemist who blesses the dough with a secret incantation.
    - This tale marks the introduction of alchemical elements into the Gingerbread Golem myth, linking it more closely to traditional golem stories.

Religious and Mythological Influences

While the Gingerbread Golem does not have direct ties to religious traditions, its early stories often draw upon themes and motifs found in religious texts and myths.

1. **The Influence of Kabbalistic Golem Lore:**
    - Early writers of Gingerbread Golem tales were likely familiar with the Jewish tradition of the clay golem. Elements such as the golem's role as a protector and its dependence on the creator's intentions are mirrored in Gingerbread Golem stories.
    - The shift from clay to gingerbread reflects a cultural adaptation, infusing the solemnity of golem myths with the festive and communal aspects of gingerbread-making.
2. **Seasonal Symbolism:**
    - The Gingerbread Golem's association with winter festivities connects it to themes of renewal, abundance, and protection, which are common in religious and mythological celebrations of the solstice.

- Its creation during times of communal gatherings emphasizes its role as a unifying figure, protecting both physical and spiritual well-being.

Early Printed Works and Popularization

With the invention of the printing press in the 15th century, stories of the Gingerbread Golem began to reach broader audiences. Early printed works often included illustrations and embellishments that helped cement the golem's place in popular imagination.

1. **Gingerbread in Chapbooks:**
   - Cheaply produced booklets called chapbooks were a popular medium for distributing folklore in the 16th and 17th centuries. Several chapbooks from this period include references to animated gingerbread figures, though not always explicitly called "golems."
   - These stories often portrayed the Gingerbread Golem as a mischievous yet ultimately benevolent figure, reflecting the lighter tone of holiday traditions.
2. **Illustrated Festive Tales:**
   - Early woodcut illustrations accompanying these tales depicted gingerbread figures with exaggerated features, such as oversized arms or glowing eyes, emphasizing their protective and magical qualities.
   - These visual representations helped establish the iconic image of the Gingerbread Golem as both whimsical and formidable.

The Role of Oral Tradition in Shaping Early Accounts

Despite the rise of written texts, oral traditions continued to shape the Gingerbread Golem myth. Communities adapted the stories to reflect local customs and concerns, resulting in a rich tapestry of variations.

1. **Regional Variations:**
    - In Scandinavian versions, the Gingerbread Golem was said to guard livestock during harsh winters.
    - In Eastern European tales, it protected families from supernatural threats, such as witches or wandering spirits.
2. **Interactive Storytelling:**
    - Many early accounts were designed to be performed or retold during festive gatherings. This interactive element allowed for the inclusion of audience participation, such as reciting blessings or mimicking the actions of a Gingerbread Golem.

Key Themes in Early Written Accounts

The early texts and stories documenting the Gingerbread Golem share several recurring themes that highlight its cultural significance.

1. **Protection and Guardianship:**
   - The Gingerbread Golem is consistently portrayed as a protector, whether guarding families, feasts, or communities.
   - This theme reflects the universal human desire for safety and the use of myth as a means of addressing fears and uncertainties.
2. **Creation and Transformation:**
   - The act of baking and animating a Gingerbread Golem symbolizes transformation, blending culinary artistry with magical intent.
   - This theme reinforces the connection between the domestic sphere and the mystical.
3. **Impermanence:**
   - The Gingerbread Golem's ephemeral nature—often crumbling to crumbs or being consumed—underscores themes of transience and renewal, aligning it with broader seasonal and mythological cycles.

Conclusion

The first written accounts of the Gingerbread Golem laid the foundation for its enduring place in folklore and festive traditions. These early texts reflect a rich interplay between oral storytelling, cultural adaptation, and the universal themes of protection and transformation. By documenting the Gingerbread Golem's early tales, scribes and storytellers ensured that this sweet yet formidable figure would continue to captivate and inspire for generations to come. The following chapters will delve deeper into the evolution and expansion of the Gingerbread Golem myth, exploring how it has been reimagined across time and cultures.

Chapter 5: Mythical Ingredients: Symbolism in Gingerbread Recipes

Analysis of Ingredients Like Ginger, Cinnamon, and Sugar in the Context of Folklore

The legend of the Gingerbread Golem owes much of its symbolic richness to the ingredients used in its creation. Gingerbread is more than just a confection; it is a medium imbued with layers of meaning derived from its components. Ingredients such as ginger, cinnamon, nutmeg, and sugar were not only prized for their flavor but also for their associations with health, protection, and mystical properties. This chapter delves into the symbolic significance of these ingredients in folklore, mythology, and cultural traditions, revealing how they contribute to the mythical narrative of the Gingerbread Golem.

The Power of Spices: A Mystical Tradition

Spices have long held a revered place in human history, valued not only for their culinary uses but also for their medicinal, symbolic, and magical properties. In medieval Europe, the spices used in gingerbread were considered luxuries and were often linked to mystical and protective qualities.

1. **Ginger: The Fiery Root**
   - **Symbolic Associations:**
     Ginger, the namesake of gingerbread, was believed to have fiery and invigorating properties. It was associated with vitality, protection, and the ability to ward off malevolent forces.
     In folklore, ginger was thought to ignite inner warmth and courage, making it an ideal ingredient for a figure meant to guard and protect.
   - **Medicinal and Mystical Uses:**
     Ginger was used as a remedy for ailments such as colds and indigestion, reinforcing its association with resilience and health. Its warming nature was thought to shield against

the literal and figurative cold of winter, aligning with the Gingerbread Golem's role as a winter guardian.

2. **Cinnamon: The Sweet Shield**
    - **Symbolic Associations:**
    Cinnamon, with its sweet and aromatic properties, symbolized abundance, prosperity, and spiritual protection. In magical traditions, it was used to ward off negative energy and attract positive influences.
    This spice added a layer of sweetness to the Gingerbread Golem's protective nature, reflecting its dual role as both a fierce guardian and a symbol of communal joy.
    - **Historical Significance:**
    In medieval Europe, cinnamon was a prized import, often associated with wealth and high status. Its inclusion in gingerbread elevated the confection to a symbol of festivity and celebration.

3. **Nutmeg: The Mysterious Enhancer**
    - **Symbolic Associations:**
    Nutmeg was associated with mystery and the unknown. Its inclusion in magical recipes was thought to enhance intuition and provide protection against unseen dangers.
    For the Gingerbread Golem, nutmeg's subtle presence represented its connection to both the mystical and the domestic realms, bridging the gap between the magical and the mundane.
    - **Medicinal and Mystical Uses:**
    Nutmeg was believed to stimulate the mind and protect against illness, reinforcing its role in the creation of a figure meant to safeguard its makers.

4. **Cloves: The Sacred Spice**
    - **Symbolic Associations:**
    Cloves were used in rituals to purify spaces and protect against harm. Their sharp, pungent aroma was believed to

repel evil spirits and negativity.

The inclusion of cloves in gingerbread tied the Golem to themes of purification and spiritual defense, enhancing its role as a protector.
- **Cultural Significance:**
  Cloves were often used in religious ceremonies and healing rituals, underscoring their sacred and protective qualities.

The Sweetness of Sugar: A Symbol of Abundance

Sugar, a key ingredient in gingerbread, holds a complex symbolism in folklore and cultural traditions. Its sweetness, rarity, and transformative properties made it a powerful symbol in both mundane and magical contexts.

1. **Symbolic Associations:**
   - Sugar was often associated with abundance, joy, and the celebration of life. Its inclusion in gingerbread symbolized the blessings of prosperity and happiness, particularly during festive seasons.
   - In magical traditions, sugar was sometimes used as an offering to spirits or deities, reinforcing its connection to goodwill and protection.
2. **Transformative Power:**
   - The process of refining sugar from raw cane or beet was seen as a metaphor for transformation, aligning with the alchemical themes inherent in the creation of the Gingerbread Golem.
   - Sugar's ability to caramelize and harden during baking mirrored the magical act of animating a lifeless form, further linking it to the Golem mythos.
3. **Historical Context:**
   - In medieval Europe, sugar was a luxury item, often reserved for special occasions and celebrations. Its presence in gin-

gerbread elevated the confection to a status symbol, reinforcing its role as a festive and mythical creation.

Honey: The Golden Elixir

Before the widespread availability of sugar, honey was the primary sweetener used in gingerbread recipes. Its golden hue and natural origins imbued it with symbolic and mystical significance.

1. **Symbolic Associations:**
    - Honey was often seen as a divine substance, linked to the gods and associated with immortality, fertility, and wisdom. Its use in gingerbread symbolized the infusion of divine blessings into the creation of the Golem.
    - The sweetness of honey also represented harmony and balance, qualities that resonated with the protective and nurturing aspects of the Gingerbread Golem.
2. **Cultural and Mythological Significance:**
    - In many cultures, honey was considered a sacred offering to deities and spirits. Its inclusion in gingerbread tied the confection to rituals of thanksgiving and celebration.
    - Honey's preservative properties also symbolized the enduring power of protection, aligning with the Golem's role as a guardian.

Flour and Eggs: The Foundation of Life

The base ingredients of gingerbread—flour and eggs—carry their own symbolic weight, representing the foundational elements of life and creation.

1. **Flour:**
     - As a product of harvested grain, flour symbolized sustenance, fertility, and the cycle of life. Its inclusion in gingerbread tied the confection to themes of growth, nourishment, and renewal.
     - In magical traditions, flour was sometimes used in rituals to create protective circles, further connecting it to the Gingerbread Golem's protective role.
2. **Eggs:**
     - Eggs were associated with potential, creation, and the spark of life. Their use in gingerbread recipes mirrored the act of animating the Golem, turning inert materials into something imbued with vitality.
     - In folklore, eggs were often used in fertility rites and protection spells, reinforcing their symbolic connection to the Golem's role as a life-giving protector.

The Role of Heat: Transformation Through Baking

The act of baking gingerbread was seen as a transformative process, akin to the alchemical act of transmutation. The heat of the oven symbolized the spark of life, bringing the Gingerbread Golem into existence.

1. **Symbolic Heat:**
    - In many myths, fire represents purification, transformation, and the essence of life. The oven, as a controlled source of heat, became a metaphorical womb for the Gingerbread Golem, completing its transformation from raw ingredients to a living guardian.
2. **Alchemical Resonance:**
    - The baking process mirrored the alchemical stages of transformation, from the "blackening" of raw dough to the "whitening" of sugar decorations, culminating in the "redness" of a finished creation. This alignment with alchemical symbolism further linked the Gingerbread Golem to mystical traditions.

Conclusion

The ingredients of gingerbread are more than just culinary components; they are carriers of profound symbolic meaning that enhances the mythical narrative of the Gingerbread Golem. From the fiery warmth of ginger to the divine sweetness of honey, each element contributes to the Golem's identity as a protector, a symbol of abundance, and a figure of transformation. By analyzing these ingredients in the context of folklore and cultural traditions, we gain a deeper understanding of the Gingerbread Golem's role as both a festive creation and a mythical construct. This chapter sets the stage for exploring how these symbolic foundations influenced the rituals and stories surrounding the Gingerbread Golem in the chapters to come.

Chapter 6: Rising Legends: The Gingerbread Golem in Medieval Europe

Stories of Gingerbread Golems Appearing in European Mythology

The medieval period in Europe was a fertile ground for the emergence and evolution of myths, particularly those blending spiritual, magical, and domestic elements. The Gingerbread Golem, an edible adaptation of the mystical golem, found its footing in this era, shaped by a confluence of cultural traditions, seasonal rituals, and evolving culinary practices. This chapter explores the rise of the Gingerbread Golem in medieval European mythology, uncovering the tales and traditions that cemented its place as a unique and enduring figure.

The Cultural Landscape of Medieval Europe

To understand the emergence of the Gingerbread Golem, it is essential to examine the societal and cultural conditions that fostered its development.

1. **The Role of Festivals and Feasts:**
   - Medieval Europe placed great emphasis on communal celebrations tied to the agricultural calendar and Christian holy days. These events often included the sharing of symbolic foods, including spiced breads and gingerbread.
   - The dark and challenging winter months heightened the importance of protective myths and rituals, making the Gingerbread Golem a timely figure during seasonal celebrations.
2. **The Influence of Golem Myths:**
   - Jewish communities in medieval Europe brought with them the tradition of the clay golem, a mystical protector created through divine intervention.
   - These stories permeated European folklore, inspiring adaptations like the Gingerbread Golem, which reflected local culinary practices and festive traditions.

3. **The Rise of Gingerbread as an Art Form:**
    - By the 13th century, gingerbread had become a popular medium for creating decorative and symbolic figures. The transition from practical spiced bread to intricately shaped confections paralleled the rise of myths that imbued these creations with magical properties.

Early Medieval Tales of the Gingerbread Golem

The first legends of the Gingerbread Golem were likely transmitted orally before being recorded in manuscripts or collections of folklore. These tales often centered around themes of protection, community, and seasonal magic.

1. **"The Baker's Guardian" (12th Century):**
    - A popular legend from Bavaria tells the story of a baker who created a life-sized gingerbread figure to protect his village from raiders.
    - According to the tale, the baker shaped the golem using a secret recipe passed down through generations. Once baked, the Gingerbread Golem came to life, chasing away the raiders and standing guard until spring.
    - This story highlights the protective role of the Gingerbread Golem and its connection to community resilience during harsh winters.
2. **"The Sweet Defender of the Yule Feast" (13th Century):**
    - A Scandinavian tale recounts the creation of a Gingerbread Golem to guard a Yule feast from a malevolent frost spirit.
    - The story describes the golem as having eyes of glazed sugar and a heart infused with warm honey, symbolizing its protective and nurturing qualities.
    - This legend ties the Gingerbread Golem to themes of abundance and the battle against winter's harshness, aligning it with broader Yule traditions.

3. **"The Spiced Avenger" (14th Century):**
    - In a French folktale, a baker creates a Gingerbread Golem to avenge the theft of his Christmas pastries. The golem is described as swift and cunning, outsmarting the thieves and recovering the stolen goods.
    - This story introduces a more mischievous and dynamic aspect of the Gingerbread Golem, reflecting the playful tone of many holiday legends.

The Gingerbread Golem in Courtly Traditions

As gingerbread artistry became more elaborate, the myth of the Gingerbread Golem gained traction among the nobility, who saw it as a blend of culinary luxury and magical intrigue.

1. **Royal Commissions and Display Pieces:**
    - Records from the courts of England and France show that royal bakers were commissioned to create elaborate gingerbread sculptures for feasts and celebrations. Some of these figures were inspired by Gingerbread Golem legends, designed to impress and entertain.
    - These creations were often adorned with gold leaf and precious spices, elevating the Gingerbread Golem to a symbol of wealth and power.
2. **Courtly Tales of Animated Gingerbread:**
    - Stories of animated gingerbread figures became popular in courtly circles, blending humor and mysticism. In one tale, a noblewoman commissions a Gingerbread Golem to guard her jewelry during a Christmas banquet, only for the golem to mistakenly chase away her guests as well.
    - Such stories reflect the duality of the Gingerbread Golem as both protector and potential source of chaos.

Regional Variations and Local Legends

The Gingerbread Golem myth adapted to the unique cultural and culinary traditions of different European regions, resulting in a rich tapestry of variations.

1. **Germanic Traditions:**
    - In Germany, the Gingerbread Golem was often linked to the concept of *lebkuchen*, a spiced honey cake. Legends described *lebkuchen* golems as protectors of the hearth, particularly during the Twelve Days of Christmas.
    - These tales emphasized the golem's role in warding off evil spirits and ensuring the prosperity of the household.
2. **Scandinavian Interpretations:**
    - Scandinavian myths often depicted the Gingerbread Golem as a guardian of livestock and farmland, protecting against both human thieves and supernatural creatures like trolls.
    - These versions of the golem were typically smaller in size, reflecting the practicality of rural life and the focus on domestic protection.
3. **Eastern European Variations:**
    - In Eastern Europe, gingerbread figures were sometimes associated with fertility and renewal, tying the Gingerbread Golem to springtime rituals as well as winter celebrations.
    - Stories from this region often included magical recipes or incantations said to bring the Gingerbread Golem to life, blending local folk magic with broader golem traditions.

Themes and Motifs in Medieval Gingerbread Golem Tales

The recurring themes and motifs in medieval Gingerbread Golem legends reveal the deeper cultural significance of these stories.

1. **Protection and Guardianship:**
    - The Gingerbread Golem is consistently portrayed as a protector, whether guarding villages, feasts, or individuals. This theme reflects the communal need for safety and stability, particularly during the unpredictable winter months.
2. **Seasonal Symbolism:**
    - The creation and animation of the Gingerbread Golem are tied to seasonal rituals, emphasizing themes of renewal, abundance, and resilience against adversity.
3. **The Dual Nature of Creation:**
    - Like traditional golems, the Gingerbread Golem embodies the duality of creation: it can be a benevolent guardian or a source of unintended chaos, depending on the intentions and actions of its creator.
4. **The Impermanence of Magic:**
    - The transient nature of gingerbread reinforces the idea that the Gingerbread Golem's magic is temporary, aligning with the cyclical nature of life and the seasons.

Conclusion

The medieval period was instrumental in shaping the myth of the Gingerbread Golem, weaving it into the cultural fabric of Europe through stories of protection, celebration, and transformation. These legends reflect the ingenuity of communities that adapted ancient golem traditions to their own culinary and festive practices. The Gingerbread Golem's rise in medieval Europe set the stage for its continued evolution, ensuring its place as both a mythical guardian and a beloved holiday symbol. In the chapters ahead, we will explore how this sweet yet formidable figure was reimagined in modern times, blending tradition with innovation.

Chapter 7: Festive Animations: The Golem and Winter Holidays

Connection to Christmas and Yule Traditions, Including Rituals and Superstitions

The Gingerbread Golem's enduring legacy is intrinsically tied to the festive traditions of winter holidays, particularly Christmas and Yule. As a symbol of protection, abundance, and the magic of creation, this mythical figure resonated with the themes and practices of these celebrations. This chapter examines how the Gingerbread Golem became an iconic part of winter festivities, exploring its connections to Christmas and Yule traditions, the rituals that brought it to life, and the superstitions that surrounded its creation and use.

Winter Holidays as a Time of Protection and Magic

The long, dark winters of medieval Europe were both a practical and symbolic challenge for communities. Winter holidays like Christmas and Yule served as a beacon of hope and celebration during this time, combining Christian and pagan elements to mark the solstice and the renewal of the year.

1. **The Need for Protection:**
   - Winter was a time of scarcity, cold, and vulnerability. Myths and rituals surrounding protective figures, such as the Gingerbread Golem, emerged as a way to safeguard homes, families, and resources from both natural and supernatural threats.
   - The Gingerbread Golem, as a seasonal guardian, became a key figure in these protective traditions, embodying the community's desire for safety and warmth.

2. **The Magic of Creation:**
    - Winter holidays celebrated the power of transformation, from the rebirth of the sun at Yule to the birth of Christ at Christmas. The act of creating a Gingerbread Golem echoed these themes, transforming simple ingredients into a figure imbued with symbolic life.

The Gingerbread Golem and Christmas Traditions

Christmas, as celebrated in medieval and early modern Europe, was a time of feasting, gift-giving, and the sharing of stories. The Gingerbread Golem became a popular subject in these traditions, blending festive cheer with magical intrigue.

1. **Feasts and the Golem's Role:**
    - In many regions, large feasts were central to Christmas celebrations. The Gingerbread Golem was often depicted as a guardian of these feasts, protecting food from being stolen by either humans or mischievous spirits.
    - Some families created small Gingerbread Golems to place on their dining tables, believing that these figures would ensure the prosperity of their meals and the safety of their homes.
2. **Gift-Giving and Symbolism:**
    - Gingerbread Golems, crafted as edible gifts, were exchanged among friends and neighbors as symbols of goodwill and protection.
    - In some stories, Gingerbread Golems were said to bring good fortune to their recipients, particularly if they were shared with others in the community.
3. **Storytelling and Entertainment:**
    - During Christmas gatherings, tales of animated Gingerbread Golems were a popular form of entertainment. These stories often had a humorous or moralistic tone,

teaching lessons about generosity, responsibility, and the consequences of one's actions.

The Gingerbread Golem and Yule Traditions

Yule, an ancient pagan celebration of the winter solstice, heavily influenced the development of Christmas traditions. The Gingerbread Golem found a natural place in Yule festivities, reflecting the holiday's focus on renewal, protection, and the interplay of light and dark.

1. **Guardianship Against the Wild Hunt:**
   - In many Yule legends, the Wild Hunt—a ghostly procession of spirits—was believed to roam the skies, posing a danger to those caught unprotected. Gingerbread Golems were said to guard homes against these spirits, serving as tangible talismans of safety.
   - Some rituals involved placing Gingerbread Golems on windowsills or hearths as offerings to appease wandering spirits and ensure the household's protection.
2. **Symbol of the Sun's Return:**
   - Yule marked the return of the sun and the promise of longer days. The Gingerbread Golem, with its warm, spiced aroma and golden-brown hue, symbolized the warmth and light of the sun.
   - Baking a Gingerbread Golem was seen as an act of invoking the sun's protective energy, aligning the figure with themes of renewal and resilience.
3. **Communal Baking Rituals:**
   - In some Yule traditions, families and communities gathered to bake gingerbread figures together. These communal rituals emphasized unity and shared purpose, with the Gingerbread Golem serving as a symbol of collective strength.

Rituals Surrounding the Gingerbread Golem

The creation of a Gingerbread Golem was often accompanied by specific rituals and practices, reflecting its dual role as a festive treat and a mythical protector.

1. **The Baking Process:**
    - The act of baking a Gingerbread Golem was imbued with symbolism, from the mixing of the dough (representing the unification of elements) to the application of heat (symbolizing the spark of life).
    - Some myths suggested that bakers recite blessings or incantations while shaping the Golem, imbuing it with protective energy.
2. **Decorative Elements:**
    - The decorations on a Gingerbread Golem were often chosen for their symbolic meaning. For example:
        - **Candy eyes:** Representing vigilance and the ability to see potential threats.
        - **Sugar crystals:** Symbolizing purity and protection.
        - **Honey glaze:** A sign of divine favor and abundance.
3. **Placement and Use:**
    - Gingerbread Golems were placed in key areas of the home, such as near the hearth or at the entrance, to ward off evil spirits and ensure the household's safety.
    - In some traditions, the Golem was consumed at the end of the holiday season, symbolizing the absorption of its protective energy by the family.

Superstitions Surrounding the Gingerbread Golem

As with any mythical figure, the Gingerbread Golem was surrounded by a variety of superstitions, reflecting the community's beliefs and fears.

1. **The Danger of Overbaking:**
    - Folklore warned against overbaking a Gingerbread Golem, as this was thought to make it brittle and prone to breaking, symbolizing a failure of its protective power.
    - A cracked or broken Golem was considered a bad omen, signaling potential misfortune in the coming year.
2. **Timing of Creation:**
    - It was believed that the Gingerbread Golem should only be baked during specific times, such as the solstice or Christmas Eve, to ensure its magical potency.
    - Baking the Golem outside of these times was thought to diminish its effectiveness or even attract misfortune.
3. **The Risk of Mischief:**
    - Some tales warned that a poorly made or improperly blessed Gingerbread Golem could become mischievous, playing pranks on its creators or failing to perform its duties.
    - This superstition emphasized the importance of intention and care in the Golem's creation.

Themes and Motifs in Festive Gingerbread Golem Stories

The Gingerbread Golem's connection to winter holidays is marked by recurring themes that reflect the cultural values and beliefs of the time.

1. **Protection and Resilience:**
    - The Golem's role as a guardian against both physical and spiritual threats underscores the communal desire for safety during the challenging winter months.
2. **Renewal and Abundance:**
    - The act of creating a Gingerbread Golem mirrors the themes of renewal and abundance central to both Christmas and Yule, emphasizing the transformative power of the season.
3. **Joy and Whimsy:**
    - Despite its protective role, the Gingerbread Golem is often depicted as a playful and endearing figure, capturing the festive spirit of the holidays.

Conclusion

The Gingerbread Golem's integration into Christmas and Yule traditions speaks to its versatility as both a mythical protector and a symbol of festive joy. Its connection to seasonal rituals and superstitions highlights the deep cultural significance of this edible creation, bridging the gap between the magical and the domestic. As we explore the evolution of the Gingerbread Golem in subsequent chapters, its role in winter holidays provides a foundation for understanding its enduring appeal and adaptability across time and traditions.

Chapter 8: Sweet Yet Savage: The Duality of the Gingerbread Golem

Examination of Its Dual Nature as a Protector and a Potential Destroyer

The Gingerbread Golem is a fascinating figure in folklore because of its dual nature—both sweet and savage. On one hand, it is a guardian and protector, created with good intentions to shield its makers from harm. On the other, it has the potential to become a force of chaos and destruction if mishandled or imbued with misguided intentions. This duality mirrors the complexity of human creation, reflecting themes of responsibility, morality, and the unintended consequences of wielding power. In this chapter, we examine the Gingerbread Golem's contrasting roles, exploring its symbolic significance as both a benevolent defender and a potential threat.

The Golem Archetype: A Foundation for Duality

The Gingerbread Golem's duality finds its roots in the broader archetype of the golem, a figure from Jewish folklore with a history of both heroism and chaos.

1. **The Protector Role:**
    - Traditional golems, such as the one in the Prague legend, were created to serve as protectors of vulnerable communities.
    - These protectors were powerful but limited in intelligence and moral reasoning, relying entirely on the intentions of their creators.
2. **The Dangers of Mismanagement:**
    - Golems, while intended as protectors, could become destructive if their creators lost control or failed to provide proper guidance.

- This theme of unintended consequences forms the foundation for the Gingerbread Golem's dual nature.
3. **The Adaptation to Gingerbread:**
    - The Gingerbread Golem inherits this duality, blending the sweetness of its confectionary medium with the latent potential for chaos that characterizes all golems.

The Sweet Protector: Benevolence in Action

As a protector, the Gingerbread Golem embodies warmth, nurturing, and selflessness. Its role as a guardian reflects humanity's desire for safety and stability during challenging times, particularly the harsh winter months.

1. **Guarding Against Threats:**
    - In many tales, the Gingerbread Golem is depicted as a benevolent force that defends its creators from harm.
    - Examples include protecting homes from thieves, warding off malevolent spirits, and safeguarding livestock during winter.
2. **A Symbol of Care and Community:**
    - The creation of a Gingerbread Golem often occurs during festive seasons, emphasizing its connection to themes of togetherness and shared responsibility.
    - Its protective role extends beyond physical safety to include fostering joy and abundance, symbolized by its sweet and fragrant form.
3. **Self-Sacrificing Nature:**
    - The Gingerbread Golem is frequently portrayed as willing to sacrifice itself for the good of its creators. For example, it might crumble to stop an intruder or be consumed to transfer its protective energy to the family.
    - This self-sacrificial element aligns with broader themes of devotion and the cyclical nature of life and death.

The Savage Destroyer: When Sweetness Turns Sour

Despite its benevolent intentions, the Gingerbread Golem can also become a source of danger. This darker aspect often emerges from flaws in its creation, misuse of its power, or unintended consequences.

1. **Flaws in Creation:**
    - Folklore warns that a poorly made Gingerbread Golem—whether due to rushed craftsmanship or impure intentions—might become unpredictable or malicious.
    - For example, a Golem with mismatched decorations (such as uneven eyes or a cracked body) might develop a mischievous or vengeful personality.
2. **Unintended Consequences:**
    - In some tales, the Gingerbread Golem's protective instincts lead to overzealous actions. For instance, it might harm innocent bystanders in its effort to eliminate perceived threats.
    - These stories reflect the dangers of unchecked power and the importance of careful guidance.
3. **Misuse of Power:**
    - The creator's intentions play a crucial role in the Golem's behavior. A Gingerbread Golem crafted with selfish or malicious motives is more likely to exhibit destructive tendencies.
    - Such tales serve as cautionary lessons about the ethical responsibilities of creators and the potential for power to corrupt.
4. **Stories of Chaos and Mischief:**
    - In lighter versions of these tales, the Gingerbread Golem causes mischief rather than outright harm. For example:
        - A Golem might rearrange furniture or eat the family's Christmas feast while trying to "guard" it.

- These humorous stories highlight the Golem's childlike simplicity and the unintended consequences of its single-minded focus.

The Balance Between Sweetness and Savagery

The Gingerbread Golem's duality is not simply a flaw but a reflection of the complex nature of creation and responsibility. Its behavior depends on the intentions and actions of its creator, emphasizing the delicate balance between sweetness and savagery.

1. **The Role of Intentions:**
    - A Gingerbread Golem crafted with pure intentions and proper rituals is more likely to fulfill its role as a benevolent protector.
    - Conversely, careless or malicious intentions can tip the balance toward chaos, turning sweetness into savagery.
2. **Symbolic Lessons:**
    - The Golem's dual nature serves as a metaphor for human creation and the consequences of wielding power without understanding its potential impact.
    - These stories often carry moral lessons about responsibility, humility, and the need for balance in all endeavors.
3. **The Role of Rituals and Blessings:**
    - Many tales emphasize the importance of rituals and blessings in shaping the Golem's character. A properly blessed Gingerbread Golem is seen as a harmonious blend of sweetness and strength, capable of fulfilling its purpose without causing harm.

Myths and Stories Exploring Duality

Numerous legends illustrate the dual nature of the Gingerbread Golem, showcasing its capacity for both protection and destruction.

1. **"The Overprotective Golem" (German Folklore):**
    - In this story, a baker creates a Gingerbread Golem to guard his family during a harsh winter. However, the Golem becomes overly protective, barring even friendly visitors from entering the home.
    - The tale underscores the importance of clear intentions and boundaries in guiding the Golem's behavior.
2. **"The Runaway Golem" (Scandinavian Tale):**
    - A Gingerbread Golem created to guard a Yule feast becomes mischievous, stealing food and hiding it from the family. The Golem ultimately learns to share and is consumed as part of the feast, symbolizing reconciliation and renewal.
3. **"The Vengeful Protector" (Eastern European Legend):**
    - A Gingerbread Golem crafted to guard a village against invaders becomes vengeful after its creator is harmed. It destroys both friend and foe in its rampage, serving as a cautionary tale about the dangers of unchecked power.

Themes and Symbolism in Duality

The duality of the Gingerbread Golem reflects deeper cultural and philosophical themes, resonating across time and traditions.

1. **The Complexity of Creation:**
   - The Golem's behavior mirrors the creator's intentions, symbolizing the moral and ethical responsibilities inherent in the act of creation.
2. **The Balance of Power:**
   - The Gingerbread Golem serves as a reminder that power, even in its sweetest form, must be guided by wisdom and restraint.
3. **The Interplay of Light and Dark:**
   - The Golem's dual nature aligns with the broader themes of winter holidays, which celebrate the balance between darkness and light, scarcity and abundance.

Conclusion

The Gingerbread Golem's duality as both protector and potential destroyer is a testament to its enduring complexity and relevance. Its stories remind us of the importance of intention, responsibility, and balance in creation, reflecting universal truths about the human condition. As we continue to explore the evolution of the Gingerbread Golem in subsequent chapters, its dual nature serves as a foundation for understanding its multifaceted role in mythology and culture. Sweet yet savage, the Gingerbread Golem remains a symbol of both humanity's aspirations and its challenges in wielding the power of creation.

Chapter 9: The Sorcerer's Recipe: Creation Rituals

Detailed Breakdown of Rituals and Chants Associated with Gingerbread Golem Creation

The creation of a Gingerbread Golem is steeped in both culinary precision and mystical ritual. Stories of these animated confections often include elaborate instructions, recipes, and chants meant to imbue the figure with life and purpose. These rituals reflect the blending of magical traditions and practical craftsmanship, emphasizing the symbolic transformation of everyday ingredients into a protector and guardian. In this chapter, we will explore the detailed steps of creating a Gingerbread Golem, focusing on the mystical elements that elevate the act of baking into a form of alchemical creation.

The Foundation: Preparing the Ritual Space

The creation of a Gingerbread Golem begins long before the dough is mixed. Folklore emphasizes the importance of intention and preparation, with many rituals prescribing specific steps to purify the space and align the creator's energy with the task at hand.

1. **Purification of the Space:**
    - **Sweeping and Cleaning:** The kitchen or workspace must be thoroughly cleaned to remove negative energy and impurities. This act symbolizes clearing the way for a harmonious creation.
    - **Incense or Herbs:** Burning cleansing herbs such as sage, rosemary, or juniper is believed to purify the air and invite protective spirits to guide the process.
2. **Setting the Mood:**
    - **Lighting Candles:** Candles are often lit in specific colors to align with the Golem's intended purpose. For example:
        - White for protection and purity.

- Gold or yellow for abundance and vitality.
- Red for strength and courage.
- **Ambient Music or Chants:** Some rituals call for the playing of soft, harmonious music or the chanting of protective prayers to create an atmosphere of focus and intention.

3. **Tools and Ingredients as Sacred Objects:**
    - The tools and ingredients used in the ritual are treated with reverence. Some traditions recommend blessing the rolling pin, cookie cutters, and mixing bowls with a simple chant or sprinkle of saltwater to imbue them with positive energy.

The Recipe: Ingredients as Symbols

Every ingredient in a Gingerbread Golem recipe carries symbolic significance, aligning with the magical purpose of the creation.

1. **Gingerbread Dough:**
    - **Ginger:** Represents warmth, protection, and vitality. It forms the "spirit" of the Golem, imbuing it with energy to ward off harm.
    - **Cinnamon and Cloves:** These spices symbolize purification and spiritual defense, protecting the Golem and its creators from negative forces.
    - **Honey or Sugar:** Sweeteners represent abundance, harmony, and goodwill, ensuring the Golem's role as a benevolent guardian.
    - **Flour and Eggs:** These foundational ingredients symbolize stability and life, anchoring the Golem to its purpose.
2. **Decorative Elements:**
    - **Candy Eyes:** Represent vigilance and the ability to detect danger. Some myths suggest using colored sugar crystals to enhance this effect.
    - **Icing Markings:** Intricate patterns drawn with icing may include protective runes, sigils, or symbols meant to amplify the Golem's power.
    - **Golden Glaze:** A final brush of honey or a shimmering glaze symbolizes divine favor and strengthens the Golem's connection to its creator.

The Ritual of Creation: Infusing the Dough

Once the ingredients are prepared, the act of mixing and shaping the dough is accompanied by chants and blessings designed to awaken the Gingerbread Golem's potential.

1. **Mixing the Dough:**
    - As the ingredients are combined, the creator recites a chant to unify the elements. A common chant from Eastern European folklore reads:

"Earth and fire, warmth and spice,
Bring protection, strong and wise.
Sweetness shields, strength defends,
Let this form serve noble ends."

-
    - The chant is repeated until the dough reaches the desired consistency, symbolizing the gradual awakening of the Golem's latent energy.

1. **Shaping the Golem:**
    - The act of rolling and cutting the dough is seen as a sacred act. Folklore suggests speaking the Golem's intended purpose aloud during this step, such as:
        - "Protect this home from harm."
        - "Guard the feast and bring us joy."

- Some traditions call for pressing a small charm or token, such as a coin or a protective amulet, into the dough as a way of personalizing the Golem.

The Animation: Baking and Chants

The moment of transformation occurs in the oven, where the Gingerbread Golem is infused with life through the application of heat. This stage is often accompanied by focused chanting and ritual observances.

1. **The Oven as a Sacred Space:**
   - The oven is treated as a metaphorical crucible, symbolizing the alchemical transformation of raw materials into a living creation.
   - Some traditions recommend tracing a protective symbol, such as a pentacle or cross, on the oven door before placing the Golem inside.
2. **Chants During Baking:**
   - As the Golem bakes, the creator recites chants to guide its transformation. A common example from Scandinavian lore is:

"Fire within, warmth without,
Breathe in life, cast fear out.
Stand to guard, stand to fight,
Protect this home through darkest night."

-
  - The chant is repeated softly until the baking process is complete, reinforcing the creator's intention.

1. **Timing and Observation:**
   - Folklore warns against overbaking the Golem, as this can lead to cracks or brittleness, symbolic of weakened protective power.
   - Some traditions involve watching the oven closely for "signs" of the Golem's readiness, such as a golden-brown hue or the aroma of spices filling the air.

Final Steps: Bringing the Golem to Life

Once baked, the Gingerbread Golem undergoes its final stage of animation through decoration and activation rituals.

1. **Decorating with Intention:**
   - Each decorative element is applied with care and purpose, often accompanied by affirmations. For example:
     - While adding candy eyes: "See all threats and keep them at bay."
     - While piping icing patterns: "These lines weave protection, these shapes hold strength."
2. **The Activation Chant:**
   - The final chant is spoken to awaken the Golem's protective spirit. A traditional verse might include:

"With spice and sweet, with heart and soul,
I awaken you to guard this goal.
Stand strong, stand true, by my command,
Protect this home, by fire and hand."

-
  - Some creators touch the Golem's "heart" (often marked with a candy or icing detail) while reciting the chant to symbolize the spark of life.

1. **Placing the Golem:**
   - The Gingerbread Golem is placed in a specific location within the home, such as near the hearth, on the dining table, or at the entrance.
   - In some traditions, the creator offers a small blessing or prayer of gratitude to finalize the ritual.

Symbolism in the Rituals

The rituals surrounding the Gingerbread Golem's creation are rich with symbolic meaning, reflecting broader themes of transformation, protection, and responsibility.

1. **The Elements in Balance:**
    - The combination of earth (flour), fire (oven), water (liquids in the dough), and air (spices) mirrors the alchemical principles of harmony and balance.
2. **Intention and Responsibility:**
    - The rituals emphasize the importance of clear intentions, reminding creators that their thoughts and actions shape the Golem's behavior and purpose.
3. **The Cycle of Life and Renewal:**
    - The eventual consumption of the Gingerbread Golem, common in many traditions, symbolizes the cyclical nature of life, protection, and renewal.

Conclusion

The rituals and chants associated with the Gingerbread Golem's creation elevate it from a simple holiday treat to a mystical guardian imbued with symbolic power. These detailed practices reflect humanity's enduring fascination with the act of creation, blending culinary art with spiritual intent. The Sorcerer's Recipe serves as a reminder of the delicate balance between craftsmanship and magic, offering a profound glimpse into the traditions that shaped the Gingerbread Golem's mythical identity. As we continue to explore its role in folklore and culture, these rituals underscore its significance as both a protector and a symbol of festive joy.

Chapter 10: Guardians of Hearth and Home
Stories of Gingerbread Golems as Protectors of Families and Villages

The Gingerbread Golem occupies a unique role in folklore as a steadfast guardian of homes and communities. Rooted in traditions of protection and resilience, the Gingerbread Golem transcends its humble, edible origins to embody the enduring human desire for safety and sanctuary. This chapter explores stories and legends where these sweet-yet-stalwart figures serve as protectors, examining their symbolic significance, the threats they defend against, and the moral lessons embedded in their tales.

The Hearth: A Symbolic Center of Protection

In many cultures, the hearth is more than a place for cooking—it is the symbolic heart of the home, representing warmth, sustenance, and protection. The Gingerbread Golem, often crafted near or placed on the hearth, reflects these values, embodying the dual role of guardian and nurturer.

1. **The Hearth as a Sacred Space:**
    - In medieval Europe, the hearth was seen as a liminal space where the physical and spiritual worlds intersected. Protecting the hearth meant safeguarding the family's well-being on multiple levels.
    - The Gingerbread Golem, baked and "born" in the hearth's heat, became a natural extension of its protective energy.
2. **Stories of Hearth Guardianship:**
    - Folktales often describe the Gingerbread Golem as a vigilant protector stationed near the hearth, watching over the family as they slept or gathered for meals.
    - In these stories, the Golem acts as both a deterrent to intruders and a spiritual shield against malevolent forces.

The Role of the Gingerbread Golem in Protecting Families

The Gingerbread Golem's role as a family protector is central to many legends, emphasizing its connection to domestic harmony and safety.

1. **"The Sweet Sentinel" (German Folklore):**
    - In this story, a baker creates a Gingerbread Golem to protect his family during a particularly harsh winter, when food shortages drive desperate neighbors to theft.
    - The Golem, stationed at the door, thwarts multiple break-in attempts, using its imposing size and the sweet-but-pungent aroma of spices to intimidate would-be thieves.
    - The tale concludes with the Golem's symbolic sacrifice, crumbling into crumbs to nourish the family during their final days of winter scarcity, highlighting its role as both protector and provider.
2. **"The Guardian of the Feast" (French Legend):**
    - A Gingerbread Golem is crafted by a grandmother to protect the family's Christmas feast from mischievous spirits.
    - The Golem is said to patrol the table, swatting away unseen hands and preventing food from spoiling.
    - This lighthearted tale underscores the importance of gratitude and the communal spirit of holiday gatherings.
3. **"The Midnight Watchman" (Scandinavian Tale):**
    - A widowed mother bakes a Gingerbread Golem to guard her children while she works nights in a nearby village.
    - The Golem stands vigil by the door, driving off wolves and even a wandering troll. Its eventual crumbling coincides with the mother's return to stability, symbolizing its mission's completion.

Gingerbread Golems as Protectors of Villages

Beyond the home, the Gingerbread Golem also appears in stories as a communal guardian, protecting entire villages from threats both natural and supernatural.

1. **"The Defender of the Winter's Gate" (Eastern European Legend):**
    - A village facing a particularly brutal winter is plagued by wolves and bandits. The townspeople, led by the local baker, create a massive Gingerbread Golem to guard the village gates.
    - The Golem's sweet scent lures away the wolves, while its formidable appearance and ability to hurl hardened chunks of gingerbread deter human intruders.
    - In the spring, the villagers break the Golem into pieces and share it as a symbol of renewal and unity.
2. **"The Spiced Protector" (English Folklore):**
    - A Gingerbread Golem is crafted to guard a village's annual Yule log ceremony from jealous neighboring towns.
    - The Golem, infused with sacred spices and adorned with protective symbols, is said to glow faintly as it patrols the village square.
    - The tale highlights the Golem's role as a figure of communal pride and its ability to foster unity against external threats.
3. **"The Baker's Army" (Central European Myth):**
    - In a time of war, a baker creates multiple Gingerbread Golems to defend his village from invaders. The Golems, animated by a secret chant, act as both soldiers and decoys, confusing the enemy and buying time for the villagers to escape.

- This story underscores the Golem's capacity for selflessness and its connection to human ingenuity in the face of adversity.

Threats the Gingerbread Golem Defends Against

The legends of the Gingerbread Golem often focus on the various dangers it is crafted to repel, each reflecting the concerns and fears of the communities that created them.

1. **Human Intruders:**
    - Many stories emphasize the Golem's role as a deterrent to thieves, raiders, or rival villagers. Its intimidating size and presence, often enhanced by symbolic decorations, make it an effective guardian.
    - In some tales, the Golem uses its sweet scent to lure intruders into a false sense of security before driving them away.
2. **Supernatural Forces:**
    - The Gingerbread Golem is often portrayed as a spiritual protector, warding off ghosts, trolls, witches, and other malevolent beings.
    - In these stories, the Golem's sweet and spicy aroma is said to repel evil, while its physical form serves as a shield against curses or hexes.
3. **Natural Threats:**
    - Tales of the Gingerbread Golem defending homes and villages from wolves, bears, and harsh weather highlight its role as a protector of physical safety.
    - These stories often emphasize the Golem's temporary nature, with its eventual crumbling or consumption symbolizing the passing of danger and the return of balance.

Themes in Guardian Stories

The stories of Gingerbread Golems as protectors reflect universal themes and values that resonate across cultures and time periods.

1. **Resilience and Ingenuity:**
    - The creation of a Gingerbread Golem often occurs in times of crisis, symbolizing the resilience and resourcefulness of individuals and communities.
2. **The Balance of Strength and Sweetness:**
    - The Golem's dual nature as both a fierce defender and a comforting presence mirrors the balance of strength and compassion required to safeguard loved ones.
3. **Sacrifice and Renewal:**
    - Many tales emphasize the Golem's self-sacrificial nature, with its eventual destruction serving as a reminder of the cyclical nature of life and the importance of renewal.
4. **Unity and Cooperation:**
    - The crafting of a Gingerbread Golem is often a communal effort, reflecting the importance of collective action in overcoming adversity.

Modern Interpretations and Legacy

While the Gingerbread Golem originated in folklore, its stories continue to inspire modern interpretations, from children's literature to holiday traditions.

1. **Holiday Decorations:**
    - Gingerbread houses and figures, often adorned with protective symbols, echo the Golem's role as a guardian of hearth and home.
2. **Symbol of Protection and Celebration:**
    - The Gingerbread Golem remains a beloved figure, embodying the enduring values of family, community, and resilience in the face of hardship.

Conclusion

The stories of Gingerbread Golems as guardians of hearth and home reflect humanity's timeless desire for protection and safety. These sweet yet powerful figures serve as symbols of resilience, unity, and the magic of creation, inspiring both cautionary tales and celebrations of communal strength. As protectors of families and villages, the Gingerbread Golem represents the best of both the magical and the mundane, bridging the gap between folklore and tradition. Through its stories, the Gingerbread Golem continues to stand watch over the hearts and homes of those who embrace its enduring legacy.

Chapter 11: The Gingerbread Wars
Myths of Armies of Gingerbread Golems in Battles of Old

The image of an army of Gingerbread Golems marching into battle is both whimsical and profound. These myths blend the sweetness of festive traditions with the gravity of conflict, using the Gingerbread Golem as a symbol of resilience, resourcefulness, and community unity in the face of overwhelming odds. Stories of Gingerbread Wars often center on themes of protection, ingenuity, and sacrifice, highlighting the role of these edible warriors in defending homes, villages, and even kingdoms. This chapter explores the legends of Gingerbread Golem armies, analyzing their origins, symbolic significance, and the tales that have made them an enduring part of folklore.

The Origins of the Gingerbread Wars

The concept of a Gingerbread Golem army likely emerged as an extension of individual protector myths, scaled up to reflect communal efforts in times of war or crisis.

1. **Historical Context:**
    - Medieval Europe was rife with conflict, from territorial skirmishes to invasions by larger forces. These struggles often inspired folklore that reimagined battles through the lens of myth and magic.
    - The Gingerbread Golem, already established as a guardian of homes and villages, naturally evolved into a figure of collective defense when communities faced existential threats.
2. **Symbolic Appeal:**
    - Gingerbread, with its association with abundance and festivity, became a symbol of resilience and hope in the face of adversity.

- The creation of Gingerbread Golem armies in myths reflects the power of unity and ingenuity, showcasing the strength of communities working together.

3. **Storytelling Traditions:**
    - The Gingerbread Wars were often recounted during winter gatherings, serving as both entertainment and moral lessons about the importance of courage, cooperation, and sacrifice.

Legends of the Gingerbread Wars

Numerous folktales recount the exploits of Gingerbread Golem armies, often portraying them as unlikely yet heroic defenders in battles against overwhelming odds.

1. "The Siege of Spicedown" (English Legend):

- **The Conflict:**

  The small village of Spicedown, known for its skilled bakers, is besieged by a band of marauders during the winter solstice. With no warriors to defend them, the villagers turn to their craft, creating an army of life-sized Gingerbread Golems to guard their homes.

- **The Battle:**

  The Golems, adorned with candy shields and armed with peppermint staffs, are animated through chants and the collective will of the villagers. They stand as an impenetrable wall against the invaders, whose weapons shatter against the Golems' hardened forms.

- **The Outcome:**

  The marauders, overwhelmed by the Golems' resilience and the villagers' unity, retreat. The villagers celebrate their victory by breaking one of the Golems into pieces and sharing it as a feast, symbolizing gratitude and renewal.

2. "The Battle of the Sugared Fields" (Germanic Folklore):

- **The Conflict:**

  In this tale, a neighboring baron demands tribute from a peaceful village, threatening to burn their crops if they refuse. The village baker, inspired by golem legends, proposes creating an army of Gingerbread Golems to resist the baron's forces.

- **The Battle:**

  The Golems, infused with protective runes and covered in golden syrup for added durability, march into the fields to confront the

baron's soldiers. Using their combined strength and the element of surprise, the Golems topple the soldiers' siege engines and force them to retreat.
- **The Outcome:**

The baron, humiliated, agrees to a truce, leaving the village in peace. The tale emphasizes the power of creativity and the ability of even the most unlikely materials to triumph when wielded with ingenuity.

3. "The Frosted Defenders of Yule" (Scandinavian Myth):

- **The Conflict:**

A Yule celebration in a remote village is interrupted by a band of frost trolls, who demand food and treasure as tribute. The villagers, desperate to protect their children and traditions, craft a battalion of Gingerbread Golems to stand against the trolls.
- **The Battle:**

The Golems, infused with the warmth of the hearth and decorated with icy-blue sugar crystals, confront the trolls at the edge of the village. The Golems' spicy scent and relentless attacks force the trolls to retreat into the mountains.
- **The Outcome:**

The story ends with the villagers sharing their remaining food and celebrating the Golems' victory, underscoring themes of resilience and communal spirit.

4. **"The Great Gingerbread Uprising" (Eastern European Legend):**

- **The Conflict:**
  In a time of famine and unrest, a corrupt lord exploits his people, hoarding food while his subjects starve. A group of rebellious villagers bakes a covert army of Gingerbread Golems to overthrow the tyrant.
- **The Battle:**
  The Golems infiltrate the lord's castle, overwhelming his guards and breaking open the storerooms. The villagers, inspired by the Golems' success, storm the castle and redistribute the food.
- **The Outcome:**
  The tale concludes with the villagers establishing a new, fairer governance, with the Gingerbread Golems remembered as symbols of justice and collective power.

The Symbolism of Gingerbread Golem Armies

The myths of Gingerbread Wars are rich with symbolism, reflecting cultural values and universal themes.

1. **Community and Cooperation:**
    - The creation of Gingerbread Golem armies requires collective effort, emphasizing the strength of unity and collaboration in overcoming adversity.
2. **Ingenuity and Resourcefulness:**
    - The use of gingerbread as a medium for defense highlights the power of creativity and innovation, demonstrating how even humble materials can become instruments of victory.
3. **Resilience in the Face of Adversity:**
    - The Golems' steadfastness in battle symbolizes the resilience of communities during times of crisis, offering hope and inspiration.
4. **Temporary Nature of Protection:**
    - The eventual destruction or consumption of the Golems reflects the impermanence of all things, serving as a reminder of the cyclical nature of life and the need for renewal.

The Role of Magic and Ritual in the Gingerbread Wars

The animation of Gingerbread Golem armies is often depicted as a sacred or mystical process, blending culinary skill with magical practice.

1. **The Power of Chants and Incantations:**
    - Rituals for animating the Golems often involve chants that unify the community's intentions and imbue the figures with life.
    - Examples include:

"With fire's warmth and earth's sweet might,
Rise and guard, defend the night.
Stand as one, unyielding, strong,
Protect our home from those who wrong."

1. **Decorative Symbols and Runes:**
    - The Golems are often adorned with protective symbols or runes, believed to enhance their strength and focus their purpose.
2. **Sacred Ingredients:**
    - The choice of ingredients, such as honey for resilience or cinnamon for courage, underscores the blending of magic and practicality in the Golems' creation.

Themes in Gingerbread War Myths

The tales of Gingerbread Golem armies resonate across cultures and time, reflecting shared values and aspirations.

1. **Courage Against the Odds:**
     - These myths celebrate the courage of ordinary people who stand against seemingly insurmountable challenges.
2. **The Power of Creation:**
     - The act of creating Gingerbread Golems symbolizes the transformative power of human ingenuity and the ability to turn vulnerability into strength.
3. **Justice and Equity:**
     - Many stories involve the Golems fighting for fairness and protecting the weak, reinforcing themes of moral responsibility and community solidarity.

Conclusion

The myths of the Gingerbread Wars are more than whimsical tales; they are profound narratives about resilience, ingenuity, and the power of collective action. Through their deeds, the armies of Gingerbread Golems embody the best of humanity's ability to adapt, create, and protect. As protectors of homes and defenders of villages, these sweet but stalwart figures continue to inspire and delight, serving as enduring symbols of hope and unity in the face of adversity.

Chapter 12: Legends of the Spiced Avenger
Tales Where the Gingerbread Golem Serves as a Hero Figure

The Gingerbread Golem is often celebrated in folklore not just as a guardian but also as a heroic figure—an embodiment of courage, sacrifice, and cleverness. These stories, which often portray the Gingerbread Golem as a "Spiced Avenger," position it as a champion of justice, a savior of the downtrodden, and a symbol of resilience against overwhelming odds. This chapter explores the myths and legends in which the Gingerbread Golem steps into the role of hero, analyzing its acts of valor, the threats it faces, and the moral lessons conveyed through its exploits.

The Heroic Archetype: The Gingerbread Golem as a Champion

In its role as a hero, the Gingerbread Golem aligns with classic archetypes of the protector, the warrior, and the avenger. However, its unique composition—an edible, festive creation—adds a layer of whimsy and accessibility to its heroism, making it a relatable and endearing figure.

1. **The Sweet Yet Strong Hero:**
    - Unlike traditional heroic figures, the Gingerbread Golem's spiced and sugary form symbolizes both strength and sweetness, reflecting the balance of power and compassion in its actions.
    - Its ephemeral nature adds poignancy to its heroism, as the Golem often sacrifices itself for the greater good.
2. **A Reluctant Hero:**
    - In many stories, the Gingerbread Golem is created for protection or utility but rises to heroism when circumstances demand it.

- This reluctant transformation underscores themes of hidden potential and the extraordinary capabilities of ordinary beings.

Heroic Tales of the Gingerbread Golem

Across cultures, the legends of the "Spiced Avenger" highlight its resourcefulness, bravery, and selflessness. Below are some of the most enduring tales.

1. "The Bakery's Champion" (French Folklore):

- **The Threat:**
A tyrannical lord imposes a harsh tax on the village, demanding bread from every household as tribute. When the baker refuses, the lord's soldiers threaten to destroy his shop.
- **The Heroic Act:**
The baker crafts a Gingerbread Golem and sends it to confront the soldiers. Using its hardened limbs and surprising agility, the Golem outmaneuvers and defeats the aggressors, forcing the lord to abandon his demands.
- **The Moral:**
This tale emphasizes the power of creativity and the importance of standing up to oppression, even with limited resources.

2. "The Midnight Rescuer" (German Legend):

- **The Threat:**
A family is kidnapped by a group of bandits who plan to hold them for ransom. Desperate, the village baker creates a Gingerbread Golem and sends it into the forest to rescue them.
- **The Heroic Act:**
The Golem uses its keen senses (enhanced by the spices in its dough) to track the bandits. In a climactic battle, it overwhelms the kidnappers and guides the family back to safety.

- **The Moral:**
  The story highlights the themes of courage and loyalty, showing how a selfless protector can overcome even the most dangerous foes.

3. **"The Spiced Avenger and the Frost King" (Scandinavian Myth):**

- **The Threat:**
  A Frost King descends upon a village during Yule, freezing crops and livestock as a punishment for a perceived insult. The villagers, fearing starvation, craft a Gingerbread Golem to confront him.
- **The Heroic Act:**
  The Golem approaches the Frost King's icy palace, its spiced aroma melting the frosty barriers. In a heated confrontation, the Golem's warmth and resilience drive the Frost King back to his domain, restoring the village's vitality.
- **The Moral:**
  This tale symbolizes the triumph of warmth and community over coldness and isolation, reinforcing the values of unity and perseverance.

4. **"The Spiced Liberator" (Eastern European Folktale):**

- **The Threat:**
  A sorcerer enslaves a village, forcing its inhabitants to work endlessly in his mines. A group of villagers, led by the baker, crafts a Gingerbread Golem to fight for their freedom.
- **The Heroic Act:**
  The Golem, infused with runes of strength and courage, storms the sorcerer's tower, defeating his magical constructs and breaking the spell binding the villagers.

- **The Moral:**
  This tale underscores the themes of justice and liberation, showing how even the most unlikely champions can lead a revolution.

Recurring Themes in Heroic Tales

The legends of the Spiced Avenger are rich with recurring themes that resonate with audiences across cultures.

1. **Sacrifice for the Greater Good:**
   - Many stories end with the Gingerbread Golem sacrificing itself, whether by crumbling in battle or being consumed to share its protective energy. This selflessness reinforces its role as a hero.
2. **Cleverness and Ingenuity:**
   - The Golem often wins battles not through brute force but through clever tactics and the resourcefulness of its creator. This highlights the value of intellect and creativity in overcoming adversity.
3. **Defending the Vulnerable:**
   - Whether rescuing kidnapped families, protecting oppressed villagers, or standing against tyrants, the Gingerbread Golem consistently champions the weak and downtrodden, embodying the values of justice and compassion.
4. **The Triumph of Unity:**
   - The creation of the Golem is often a communal effort, emphasizing the strength that comes from working together toward a common goal.

The Symbolism of the Spiced Avenger

The heroic tales of the Gingerbread Golem carry rich symbolism that speaks to universal values and ideals.

1. **Strength in Sweetness:**
    - The Golem's sugary composition symbolizes the idea that even something gentle and kind can possess great strength when needed.
2. **The Balance of Power and Vulnerability:**
    - The Golem's temporary nature reminds us of the fleeting but impactful nature of heroism, where even a short-lived act can create lasting change.
3. **A Reflection of Human Potential:**
    - The Gingerbread Golem often reflects the potential within all individuals to rise to heroic challenges, despite humble origins or limitations.
4. **Seasonal Themes:**
    - The Golem's association with winter holidays ties its heroism to themes of renewal, hope, and the triumph of light over darkness.

The Gingerbread Golem as a Modern Hero

While rooted in folklore, the Spiced Avenger continues to inspire modern interpretations, from children's literature to animated films. Its adaptability as a hero figure ensures its continued relevance and appeal.

1. **Hero for All Ages:**
   - The Gingerbread Golem's sweet and approachable nature makes it an accessible hero for children, while its underlying themes of justice and sacrifice resonate with adults.
2. **Symbol of Festive Courage:**
   - The Golem's heroic tales are often revisited during the holiday season, reinforcing the values of generosity, courage, and resilience in times of hardship.

Conclusion

The legends of the Spiced Avenger elevate the Gingerbread Golem from a passive protector to an active hero, showcasing its capacity for courage, cleverness, and sacrifice. These tales remind us that heroism often comes from the most unexpected places and that even the humblest creations can rise to greatness. Through its valor and enduring symbolism, the Gingerbread Golem continues to inspire as a champion of justice, a defender of the vulnerable, and a beacon of hope in the face of adversity.

Chapter 13: Bakers and Sorcerers: The Golem-Makers
Profiles of Figures Associated with Gingerbread Golem Creation

The creation of the Gingerbread Golem is a fascinating intersection of culinary craftsmanship and mystical ritual, often attributed to remarkable individuals with a unique blend of skills and intentions. From humble bakers to enigmatic sorcerers, the figures behind the Gingerbread Golem legends embody the values, fears, and aspirations of their communities. This chapter profiles the key figures associated with the creation of these mythical protectors, examining their roles, motivations, and the legacy of their craft.

The Role of Bakers: Culinary Alchemists

In many tales, the creation of a Gingerbread Golem is credited to bakers, who combine their culinary expertise with a deep understanding of symbolism and ritual. Bakers occupy a central role in these stories as community caretakers and unlikely heroes.

1. The Village Baker: Guardian of Tradition

- **Profile:**
  The archetypal village baker appears in numerous Gingerbread Golem legends, often portrayed as a resourceful and compassionate figure who uses their craft to protect their community.
- **Key Traits:**
  - Deep connection to the community.
  - Exceptional skill in baking and decorating gingerbread.
  - Knowledge of folklore and protective rituals.
- **Example Story:**
  In the German tale *"The Defender of Spicedown,"* the village baker creates a life-sized Gingerbread Golem to guard the village from

marauding bandits. The baker's ingenuity and selflessness are celebrated as key to the community's survival.

- **Legacy:**
The village baker symbolizes the power of ordinary individuals to rise to extraordinary challenges, using their everyday skills to achieve heroic outcomes.

2. The Festive Artisan: Master of Celebration and Protection

- **Profile:**
This figure specializes in crafting intricate gingerbread figures for festivals and celebrations, imbuing them with protective qualities through artistic design and symbolic decoration.
- **Key Traits:**
    - Mastery of gingerbread artistry, including the use of edible paints, gold leaf, and intricate patterns.
    - An understanding of seasonal symbolism and its connection to protection.
- **Example Story:**
In the French legend *"The Guardian of the Feast,"* a festive artisan bakes a Gingerbread Golem adorned with sacred symbols to protect a Christmas banquet from mischievous spirits.
- **Legacy:**
Festive artisans highlight the intersection of beauty and function, demonstrating how art and tradition can serve as tools of resilience.

The Role of Sorcerers: Mystical Innovators

While bakers are the most common creators of Gingerbread Golems, some stories attribute their creation to sorcerers, alchemists, or other mystical figures who infuse the Golems with life through magical means.

1. The Hearth Sorcerer: Alchemical Innovator

- **Profile:**
  The hearth sorcerer is a magical figure who specializes in blending culinary arts with mystical practices, often viewed as a bridge between the mundane and the supernatural.
- **Key Traits:**
  - Expertise in alchemy and the symbolic properties of ingredients.
  - Ability to infuse inanimate objects with life through incantations and rituals.
- **Example Story:**
  In the Scandinavian tale *"The Frost King's Challenger,"* a hearth sorcerer assists a village in crafting a Gingerbread Golem to confront a malevolent frost spirit. The sorcerer uses a secret chant and a special blend of spices to animate the Golem and imbue it with warmth and strength.
- **Legacy:**
  The hearth sorcerer underscores the magical potential of everyday materials, illustrating how knowledge and creativity can transform the ordinary into the extraordinary.

2. The Wandering Alchemist: Keeper of Secret Recipes

- **Profile:**
  The wandering alchemist is a mysterious figure who appears in times of need, offering their expertise to help communities create Gingerbread Golems for protection or justice.
- **Key Traits:**
  - Possesses rare and secretive knowledge, including unique recipes and chants.
  - Often depicted as a morally ambiguous figure whose motives remain unclear.
- **Example Story:**
  In the Eastern European legend *"The Spiced Liberator,"* a wandering alchemist teaches an oppressed village how to craft a battalion of Gingerbread Golems to overthrow their tyrannical ruler. The alchemist disappears after the victory, leaving behind only the recipe as a legacy.
- **Legacy:**
  The wandering alchemist represents the enigmatic power of knowledge and the ethical dilemmas that often accompany its use.

Hybrid Figures: The Baker-Sorcerer

In some tales, the creator of the Gingerbread Golem embodies both roles, combining the practical skills of a baker with the mystical abilities of a sorcerer. These hybrid figures often play pivotal roles in the most complex and fantastical legends.

1. The Baker-Sorcerer of the Winter Solstice

- **Profile:**

  A revered figure in Central European folklore, the Baker-Sorcerer of the Winter Solstice is said to appear only during the darkest nights of the year, helping communities craft Gingerbread Golems to ward off supernatural threats.

- **Key Traits:**
    - Mastery of both baking and magical practices.
    - Deep understanding of seasonal cycles and their symbolic significance.

- **Example Story:**

  In the tale *"The Solstice Sentinel,"* the Baker-Sorcerer guides a village in creating a Gingerbread Golem infused with protective runes to guard against the Wild Hunt. The Golem's success ensures the village's safety until the sun's return.

- **Legacy:**

  The Baker-Sorcerer symbolizes the harmonious integration of practical skills and mystical knowledge, demonstrating the power of interdisciplinary expertise.

2. The Artisan-Mage of Yule

- **Profile:**
A figure renowned for creating decorative yet functional Gingerbread Golems during Yule celebrations, blending festive artistry with magical protection.
- **Key Traits:**
    - Artistic talent and attention to detail in crafting gingerbread figures.
    - Ability to enchant the Golems with specific traits, such as heightened vigilance or increased strength.
- **Example Story:**
In the English legend *"The Guardian of Yule Gifts,"* the Artisan-Mage crafts a Gingerbread Golem to protect children's gifts from being stolen by a mischievous sprite. The Golem not only defends the gifts but also captures the sprite, teaching it to respect the holiday spirit.
- **Legacy:**
The Artisan-Mage reflects the balance between festivity and function, illustrating how celebration and protection can coexist.

Themes in the Stories of Golem-Makers

The creators of Gingerbread Golems are central to the legends, embodying key themes that resonate across cultures and time.

1. **Ingenuity and Resourcefulness:**
    - The Golem-makers demonstrate how creativity and skill can overcome even the most daunting challenges.
2. **Community and Collaboration:**
    - Many stories emphasize the collaborative nature of Golem creation, with bakers, sorcerers, and villagers working together to achieve a common goal.
3. **The Ethical Use of Power:**
    - The creators often face moral dilemmas, reflecting the responsibility that comes with wielding transformative power.
4. **Transformation and Sacrifice:**
    - The act of creating a Gingerbread Golem often involves personal or communal sacrifice, underscoring the themes of resilience and renewal.

The Legacy of the Golem-Makers

The figures associated with the creation of Gingerbread Golems leave behind enduring legacies, inspiring both folklore and modern traditions.

1. **Cultural Heroes:**
    - Bakers and sorcerers are celebrated as cultural heroes, their stories serving as reminders of the power of creativity and courage.
2. **Festive Traditions:**
    - The rituals and practices associated with Golem creation continue to influence holiday customs, from the crafting of gingerbread houses to the decoration of festive cookies.
3. **Modern Interpretations:**
    - In contemporary storytelling, the Golem-makers are reimagined as inventors, artists, and even chefs, blending tradition with innovation.

Conclusion

The creators of Gingerbread Golems—whether humble bakers, mystical sorcerers, or a fusion of both—are the heart of these enduring legends. Their ingenuity, courage, and dedication transform simple ingredients into extraordinary protectors, embodying the values of resilience, community, and hope. Through their stories, the Golem-makers remind us of the profound impact that individuals and their creations can have, inspiring both myth and tradition for generations to come.

Chapter 14: The Gingerbread Golem in Modern Mythology
Continuation of the Myth in Modern Storytelling and Pop Culture

The Gingerbread Golem, a figure deeply rooted in the traditions of folklore and winter festivals, has undergone significant evolution in modern times. While its origins lie in protective and mystical roles within medieval Europe, the Gingerbread Golem has found new life in literature, film, television, and other aspects of popular culture. This chapter explores how the Gingerbread Golem myth has been reimagined in contemporary storytelling, highlighting its enduring appeal and adaptability to modern themes and audiences.

The Transition to Modern Mythology

The Gingerbread Golem's journey from folklore to modern mythology reflects broader cultural shifts and the evolving role of traditional narratives.

1. **From Protector to Pop Culture Icon:**
   - In its traditional form, the Gingerbread Golem served as a protector of homes and communities. Modern interpretations often emphasize its whimsical and fantastical elements, making it a popular subject for holiday-themed stories and media.
   - The character has transformed into a symbol of nostalgia, humor, and resilience, resonating with audiences of all ages.

2. **Adaptability of the Myth:**
   - The Gingerbread Golem's dual nature as both protector and potential mischief-maker allows for diverse storytelling possibilities, ranging from heroic tales to lighthearted comedies.
   - Its association with winter holidays makes it a recurring figure in seasonal narratives, while its broader themes of

creation and transformation extend its relevance beyond festive settings.

The Gingerbread Golem in Literature

Modern literature has embraced the Gingerbread Golem as a versatile character, appearing in genres ranging from fantasy to children's books.

1. **Children's Literature:**
    - The Gingerbread Golem often features as a magical and playful companion in children's stories. For example:
        - **"Ginger Guardian":** A popular children's book series about a Gingerbread Golem who protects a small village from winter monsters while teaching lessons about kindness and courage.
        - **"The Mischievous Golem":** A humorous tale where a Gingerbread Golem, intended as a protector, inadvertently causes chaos before ultimately saving the day.
    - These stories emphasize themes of friendship, responsibility, and the importance of community.
2. **Fantasy and Urban Fiction:**
    - In fantasy novels, the Gingerbread Golem often takes on a more complex role, serving as an enchanted creation or a magical ally. For instance:
        - In one urban fantasy novel, a Gingerbread Golem is animated by a modern-day alchemist to protect a bakery from corporate greed, blending traditional folklore with contemporary themes.

- Another fantasy epic portrays the Golem as part of a larger army of magical constructs, used in a climactic battle between good and evil.

3. **Poetry and Short Stories:**
    - Modern poets and short story writers often use the Gingerbread Golem as a metaphor for themes such as impermanence, sacrifice, and the interplay between sweetness and strength.

The Gingerbread Golem in Film and Television

Film and television have played a significant role in popularizing the Gingerbread Golem, particularly during the holiday season.

1. **Holiday Specials and Animated Features:**
    - The Gingerbread Golem is a frequent character in holiday specials, often portrayed as a humorous and endearing figure.
        - In one animated special, "The Golem's Gift," a Gingerbread Golem helps a young boy rediscover the meaning of family and togetherness during Christmas.
        - Another holiday movie features a Gingerbread Golem saving Santa's workshop from a mischievous elf rebellion.
2. **Fantasy and Adventure Series:**
    - The Golem has appeared in several fantasy-themed television series as a magical creation brought to life to assist heroes in their quests.
        - In one series, a Gingerbread Golem is a temporary ally, helping the protagonists navigate a winter-themed magical realm.
        - Another show reimagines the Golem as a misunderstood antihero, grappling with its creator's questionable intentions.
3. **Comedic and Satirical Depictions:**
    - In comedic interpretations, the Gingerbread Golem is often used for parody or satire, emphasizing its absurdity while retaining its charm.
        - One notable example includes a sketch comedy show where a Gingerbread Golem becomes a reluc-

tant participant in a baking competition, hilariously clashing with human contestants.

The Gingerbread Golem in Gaming

The Gingerbread Golem has also found a home in the world of gaming, where its magical and whimsical nature makes it a compelling character.

1. **Role-Playing Games (RPGs):**
    - In tabletop RPGs, the Gingerbread Golem often serves as a holiday-themed creature, complete with unique abilities such as:
        - **Sugarcoat Shield:** A defensive ability where the Golem hardens its sugary exterior to deflect attacks.
        - **Spice Burst:** A magical attack that releases a burst of cinnamon and nutmeg, temporarily stunning enemies.
    - Players can encounter the Golem as a protector of festive realms or as an ally in holiday-themed campaigns.
2. **Video Games:**
    - The Golem appears as a playable character or enemy in several holiday-themed video games.
        - In one popular game, players control a Gingerbread Golem to defend a village from waves of winter monsters.
        - Another game features the Golem as a crafting project, requiring players to gather ingredients and perform rituals to bring it to life.

The Gingerbread Golem in Modern Art and Merchandise

The Gingerbread Golem's whimsical appeal has inspired artists, crafters, and entrepreneurs, leading to a wide range of creative interpretations and products.

1. **Visual Art:**
    - Modern artists often depict the Gingerbread Golem in festive or fantastical settings, blending traditional aesthetics with contemporary styles.
    - These artworks are popular in galleries, holiday markets, and online platforms, where they capture the imagination of audiences.
2. **Holiday Merchandise:**
    - The Golem has become a staple of holiday merchandise, appearing on ornaments, greeting cards, and themed baking kits.
    - Gingerbread Golem plush toys, action figures, and collectible figurines are especially popular among children and holiday enthusiasts.
3. **Culinary Innovations:**
    - Bakers and chefs continue to innovate with Gingerbread Golem-inspired creations, from life-sized sculptures displayed at holiday events to themed cakes and cookies.

Themes in Modern Interpretations

The continued popularity of the Gingerbread Golem in modern storytelling and pop culture reflects its ability to embody timeless themes while adapting to contemporary contexts.

1. **Resilience and Protection:**
    - The Golem's role as a protector remains central, resonating with audiences seeking stories of courage and safety in uncertain times.
2. **Whimsy and Joy:**
    - The Golem's playful and festive nature brings joy to holiday celebrations, emphasizing themes of togetherness and celebration.
3. **Creativity and Innovation:**
    - The act of creating a Gingerbread Golem symbolizes human ingenuity and the transformative power of imagination, inspiring audiences to embrace their creative potential.
4. **The Balance of Sweetness and Strength:**
    - Modern portrayals continue to explore the Golem's duality, reflecting the complexity of heroism, responsibility, and the interplay of light and dark.

Conclusion

The Gingerbread Golem's enduring presence in modern mythology and pop culture speaks to its adaptability and universal appeal. From literature and film to gaming and art, the Golem has transcended its folkloric origins to become a beloved symbol of courage, creativity, and festive cheer. As it continues to inspire new stories and traditions, the Gingerbread Golem reminds us of the power of myths to evolve and resonate with each generation, blending the sweet with the extraordinary in ways that captivate the imagination.

Chapter 15: Cross-Cultural Comparisons
Similar Constructs in Other Cultures: Edible Effigies and Protective Spirits

The Gingerbread Golem is a unique blend of European folklore, festive traditions, and culinary artistry, but it is not the only cultural figure that merges food, ritual, and protection. Across the world, various cultures have developed edible effigies, protective spirits, and symbolic creations that reflect similar themes of transformation, guardianship, and celebration. This chapter explores these parallels, highlighting how different societies use food and rituals to create symbolic constructs and protect their communities.

Edible Effigies Across Cultures

Edible effigies—figures crafted from food for ritualistic or symbolic purposes—are a recurring motif in global traditions. These creations, often tied to seasonal festivals or spiritual practices, share thematic similarities with the Gingerbread Golem.

1. The Day of the Dead Sugar Skulls (Mexico):

- **Cultural Context:**
  During Día de los Muertos (Day of the Dead), sugar skulls (*calaveras de azúcar*) are crafted as offerings for deceased loved ones. These vibrant, edible creations represent the fusion of life, death, and remembrance.
- **Similarities to the Gingerbread Golem:**
    - Both are crafted from sweet, symbolic materials.
    - Sugar skulls serve as spiritual offerings, while Gingerbread Golems act as protectors, but both are tied to themes of transformation and honoring the past.
    - Decoration plays a central role in their meaning, with intricate designs enhancing their symbolic potency.

2. Marzipan Figures (Europe):

- **Cultural Context:**
Marzipan, a confection made from almonds and sugar, is molded into various shapes for Christmas and other celebrations across Europe. These figures often depict animals, people, or symbolic objects.
- **Similarities to the Gingerbread Golem:**
    - Marzipan figures are both decorative and edible, blending artistic and festive traditions.
    - Like the Gingerbread Golem, marzipan creations are associated with joy, abundance, and communal celebrations.

3. Bread Dolls (Eastern Europe):

- **Cultural Context:**
In many Slavic traditions, bread is shaped into human or animal figures for harvest festivals and protective rituals. These bread dolls symbolize fertility, protection, and the cyclical nature of life.
- **Similarities to the Gingerbread Golem:**
    - Bread dolls and Gingerbread Golems share a connection to sustenance and protection.
    - Both are temporary creations, intended to fulfill a specific ritual purpose before being consumed or returning to nature.

Protective Spirits and Constructs in Global Mythology

Beyond edible effigies, many cultures have myths and rituals involving protective spirits or constructs created to guard communities, homes, or individuals. These figures often share thematic and symbolic connections with the Gingerbread Golem.

1. The Golem (Jewish Tradition):

- **Cultural Context:**
  The original golem, a figure from Jewish mysticism, is a humanoid construct made from clay and brought to life through sacred rituals. Golems are typically created to protect communities from harm.
- **Similarities to the Gingerbread Golem:**
  - Both are constructed for protection, emphasizing the creator's intentions and moral responsibility.
  - The Gingerbread Golem is an edible reinterpretation of the clay golem, adapted to the festive and culinary traditions of Europe.
  - Both reflect themes of impermanence, as golems return to their base materials after fulfilling their purpose.

2. Zashiki-warashi (Japan):

- **Cultural Context:**
  The Zashiki-warashi are childlike spirits believed to inhabit homes, bringing good fortune and protection to the families they watch over. While not constructed, they are symbolic guardians closely tied to domestic life.
- **Similarities to the Gingerbread Golem:**

- Both are protectors of homes and families, tied to domestic spaces.
- Like the Gingerbread Golem, Zashiki-warashi are often depicted with a dual nature, capable of mischief if disrespected.

3. The Tara-Bogdan (Bulgaria):

- **Cultural Context:**
In Bulgarian folklore, the Tara-Bogdan are bread effigies made to represent protective spirits during times of famine or hardship. These figures are imbued with prayers and placed in the home or fields.
- **Similarities to the Gingerbread Golem:**
    - Both are crafted from food and serve protective roles.
    - Rituals surrounding the Tara-Bogdan emphasize the connection between sustenance, spirituality, and communal resilience, mirroring the symbolic significance of the Gingerbread Golem.

4. The Kachina Dolls (Hopi Tribe, North America):

- **Cultural Context:**
Kachina dolls are crafted by the Hopi people to represent spiritual beings that bring blessings, protection, and guidance. While traditionally made from wood, their symbolic role as protectors aligns with the Gingerbread Golem's purpose.
- **Similarities to the Gingerbread Golem:**
    - Both are physical representations of protective forces, created to bridge the spiritual and physical realms.
    - Kachina dolls, like Gingerbread Golems, are crafted with great care and intention, emphasizing their sacred purpose.

Thematic Parallels in Cross-Cultural Constructs

The Gingerbread Golem shares key themes and symbolic elements with similar constructs in other cultures, reflecting universal human concerns and values.

1. Protection and Guardianship:

- Across cultures, edible effigies and protective constructs are created to safeguard communities, homes, or individuals from harm.
- The Gingerbread Golem's role as a guardian aligns with these universal themes, emphasizing the need for safety and security.

2. Transformation and Ritual:

- Many constructs, like the Gingerbread Golem, undergo a transformative process during their creation, symbolizing the act of imbuing life or purpose into inanimate materials.
- Rituals surrounding their creation often blend practical skills (baking, crafting) with spiritual or symbolic practices.

3. Ephemeral Nature:

- Whether consumed, broken, or returned to nature, these constructs are inherently temporary, reinforcing themes of impermanence and renewal.
- The Gingerbread Golem's eventual crumbling or consumption reflects this cyclical perspective, shared by many edible effigies and protective figures.

4. Community and Collaboration:

- The creation of these constructs often involves collective effort, symbolizing the strength of unity and shared purpose.

- Like bread dolls, Kachina dolls, or sugar skulls, the Gingerbread Golem embodies the idea that community collaboration can overcome adversity.

Modern Interpretations and Cross-Cultural Influence

In today's interconnected world, the motifs and themes associated with constructs like the Gingerbread Golem have inspired cross-cultural adaptations and modern interpretations.

1. **Fusion Traditions:**
    - Modern holiday celebrations often incorporate elements from multiple cultures, blending the Gingerbread Golem with practices like crafting sugar skulls or decorating marzipan figures.
2. **Global Storytelling:**
    - Contemporary media frequently draws on cross-cultural influences, reimagining constructs like the Gingerbread Golem alongside figures such as golems, spirits, or animated effigies from other traditions.
3. **Art and Culinary Innovation:**
    - Artists and chefs experiment with blending traditions, creating edible constructs that borrow elements from various cultures, such as marzipan Golems or gingerbread Kachinas.

Conclusion

The Gingerbread Golem is part of a broader global tradition of edible effigies and protective constructs, reflecting humanity's shared concerns with safety, transformation, and community. By examining these cross-cultural parallels, we gain a deeper understanding of the universal values that underpin the Gingerbread Golem's mythology and its enduring appeal. As a sweet yet powerful protector, the Gingerbread Golem continues to resonate across cultures, inspiring both traditional practices and modern interpretations that celebrate the interplay of creativity, ritual, and resilience.

Chapter 16: Sugar and Sin: Morality in Golem Tales

Themes of Punishment, Redemption, and Morality in Gingerbread Golem Stories

The Gingerbread Golem, like many mythical constructs, serves not only as a protector but also as a mirror for human values and ethics. Its stories often explore themes of morality, casting the Golem as both an agent of justice and a cautionary figure that reflects the intentions of its creator. These tales delve into the dualities of good and evil, punishment and redemption, and the consequences of hubris and humility. In this chapter, we examine how Gingerbread Golem stories convey moral lessons, exploring their themes of sin, virtue, and the ethical dilemmas inherent in creating a powerful being.

The Golem as a Moral Mirror

The Gingerbread Golem's behavior is often tied to the moral character and intentions of its creator, making it a reflection of human values and flaws.

1. **A Vessel for Intentions:**
    - In many stories, the Gingerbread Golem behaves according to the motivations of its maker. A creator with pure intentions produces a benevolent Golem, while selfish or malicious intentions result in a destructive one.
    - This dynamic underscores the moral responsibility of creation, highlighting the idea that power should be wielded wisely and ethically.
2. **Symbolism of Sweetness and Sin:**
    - The Golem's sugary composition symbolizes human potential for kindness, generosity, and creativity. However, its potential for chaos represents the darker impulses of greed, arrogance, and lack of foresight.

- The duality of the Golem serves as a metaphor for the complexity of human morality, blending sweetness with the potential for sin.

Themes of Punishment in Gingerbread Golem Tales

The Gingerbread Golem frequently acts as an agent of justice, punishing wrongdoers or delivering karmic retribution. These tales often emphasize the consequences of unethical behavior.

1. The Vengeful Golem:

- **Example Story:**

  In the Eastern European tale *"The Bitter Sweetness of Greed,"* a merchant creates a Gingerbread Golem to guard his ill-gotten wealth. When the Golem learns of its master's deceit, it turns against him, scattering his riches to the poor before crumbling into dust.

- **Moral Lesson:**

  This story highlights the corrupting influence of greed and the inevitability of justice. The Golem becomes a metaphor for the consequences of selfishness, demonstrating that power without virtue leads to downfall.

2. The Overzealous Protector:

- **Example Story:**

  In the German legend *"The Golem's Judgment,"* a baker creates a Gingerbread Golem to guard his shop. However, when a hungry child attempts to steal a loaf of bread, the Golem's harsh punishment sparks outrage in the village. The baker, realizing his mistake, reprograms the Golem to protect with compassion rather than aggression.

- **Moral Lesson:**

    This tale emphasizes the importance of tempering justice with mercy, showing that punishment without understanding can cause harm rather than healing.

3. Punishing the Wicked:

- **Example Story:**

    In *"The Avenging Sweetness,"* a Gingerbread Golem crafted by a village elder is sent to confront a cruel noble who exploits the poor. The Golem tricks the noble into confessing his misdeeds, forcing him to atone by redistributing his wealth.

- **Moral Lesson:**

    The story reflects the idea that true justice is restorative, offering wrongdoers an opportunity for redemption while protecting the innocent.

Themes of Redemption in Gingerbread Golem Tales

While some Gingerbread Golems deliver punishment, others serve as catalysts for redemption, guiding characters toward self-improvement and moral clarity.

1. Redemption Through Sacrifice:

- **Example Story:**

    In the Scandinavian tale *"The Golem's Gift,"* a Gingerbread Golem sacrifices itself to save its creator from a winter storm, crumbling into crumbs that nourish the creator and keep them alive until rescue arrives. The creator, previously selfish and ungrateful, learns the value of generosity and vows to live a more selfless life.

- **Moral Lesson:**

    This story portrays the Golem as a Christ-like figure, whose sacrifice inspires redemption and transformation in others.

2. Guiding the Creator to Wisdom:

- **Example Story:**
  In the French legend *"The Sweet Mentor,"* a Gingerbread Golem crafted by a young apprentice baker becomes a source of guidance, teaching its creator patience, responsibility, and the importance of community.
- **Moral Lesson:**
  The tale highlights the idea that true strength lies not in power but in the wisdom to use it responsibly, with the Golem acting as a moral compass for its maker.

3. Redeeming the Golem Itself:

- **Example Story:**
  In the English tale *"The Mischievous Golem's Redemption,"* a Gingerbread Golem, initially prone to pranks and chaos, redeems itself by saving the village from an invading force. Its final act of heroism earns the gratitude and forgiveness of the community.
- **Moral Lesson:**
  This story explores the idea that even flawed beings can achieve redemption through noble actions, reflecting the universal potential for growth and change.

Ethical Dilemmas in Golem Creation

The act of creating a Gingerbread Golem often raises ethical questions about the responsibilities and consequences of wielding power.

1. The Creator's Responsibility:

- Stories frequently emphasize the importance of intention, suggesting that creators bear moral responsibility for the actions of their creations.
- For example, a careless or selfish creator might produce a destructive Golem, while a thoughtful and ethical creator ensures their Golem acts with integrity.

2. The Limits of Control:

- Many tales explore the dangers of hubris, showing how creators who seek to dominate or misuse their Golems often lose control, leading to unintended consequences.
- This theme serves as a cautionary reminder that power, even in the form of a Gingerbread Golem, must be wielded with humility and respect.

3. The Balance of Justice and Compassion:

- The Gingerbread Golem's role as an enforcer of justice often raises questions about the balance between punishment and mercy.

- Tales that explore this tension encourage audiences to consider the ethical complexities of justice and the importance of empathy in addressing wrongdoing.

Symbolism of Morality in Golem Tales

The Gingerbread Golem's composition and behavior are rich with symbolic meaning, reflecting broader themes of morality and human nature.

1. **The Duality of Sweetness and Strength:**
   - The Golem's sugary form symbolizes human potential for kindness and generosity, while its strength represents the power of justice.
   - This duality reflects the idea that morality requires a balance between compassion and accountability.
2. **Impermanence and Redemption:**
   - The temporary nature of the Gingerbread Golem underscores the fleeting nature of both sin and redemption, suggesting that moral growth is an ongoing process.
3. **Creation as Reflection:**
   - The Golem's behavior mirrors the values and intentions of its creator, emphasizing the interconnectedness of action, consequence, and responsibility.

Modern Morality in Gingerbread Golem Stories

Contemporary retellings of Gingerbread Golem tales often adapt their moral lessons to reflect modern values and challenges.

1. **Themes of Social Justice:**
   - Modern stories frequently portray the Golem as a champion of marginalized communities, addressing issues such as inequality, corruption, and environmental degradation.
2. **Exploration of Ethical Technology:**

- Some adaptations use the Golem as a metaphor for artificial intelligence or other advanced technologies, exploring the ethical dilemmas of creating powerful constructs with the potential for both good and harm.

3. **Focus on Personal Growth:**
    - Recent interpretations often emphasize the Golem's role in guiding its creator or community toward self-improvement, reflecting contemporary themes of personal responsibility and collective well-being.

Conclusion

The themes of punishment, redemption, and morality in Gingerbread Golem stories highlight the enduring relevance of these tales as vehicles for ethical exploration. Whether acting as an agent of justice, a catalyst for redemption, or a reflection of its creator's intentions, the Golem serves as a powerful metaphor for the complexities of human morality. Through its sweet yet strong form, the Gingerbread Golem reminds us of the importance of balancing justice with compassion, wielding power responsibly, and embracing the potential for growth and redemption in ourselves and others.

Chapter 17: The Vanishing Golem: Mystical Endings
Stories About the Destruction or Disappearance of Gingerbread Golems

The stories of Gingerbread Golems often conclude with their destruction or mysterious disappearance, underscoring their ephemeral nature and the impermanence of magical creations. These mystical endings are rich with symbolic meaning, reflecting themes of sacrifice, renewal, and the cyclical nature of life. Whether through self-sacrifice, natural decay, or a magical vanishing act, the Gingerbread Golem's final moments often serve as the moral or emotional climax of its story. In this chapter, we delve into the various ways these sweet protectors meet their end and the deeper significance of their departures.

The Purposeful Sacrifice

One of the most common motifs in Gingerbread Golem tales is its voluntary destruction for the greater good, often cementing its role as a selfless protector or redeemer.

1. Crumbling to Protect Its Creator

- **Example Story:**
  In the Scandinavian tale *"The Golem's Shield,"* a Gingerbread Golem stands between its creator and an attacking frost troll. Though it is shattered in the fight, its sacrifice drives the troll away, saving the village.
- **Symbolic Meaning:**
    - The act of crumbling represents the ultimate expression of loyalty and devotion.
    - The Golem's destruction is a reminder that true heroism often requires selflessness.

2. Dissolving to Save a Community

- **Example Story:**
  In the French legend *"The Sweet Torrent,"* a Gingerbread Golem, faced with a magical drought, crumbles into a stream, its sugary remains turning the water sweet and potable, saving the village from thirst.
- **Symbolic Meaning:**
  - The dissolution of the Golem into the water symbolizes transformation and renewal.
  - It serves as a metaphor for the blending of the magical and mundane to restore balance.

3. Offering Itself as Sustenance

- **Example Story:**
  In *"The Baker's Golem,"* a Gingerbread Golem sacrifices itself by crumbling into crumbs to feed a starving family. Its destruction ensures the survival of its creator and community.
- **Symbolic Meaning:**
  - This tale reflects themes of nourishment and sacrifice, tying the Golem's edible nature to its protective purpose.
  - It emphasizes the idea that even temporary creations can have lasting impacts.

Natural Decay: Returning to the Earth

In some stories, the Gingerbread Golem simply succumbs to the passage of time, crumbling or decaying as its purpose is fulfilled.

1. Erosion by Nature

- **Example Story:**
  In *"The Golem of the Winter's Edge,"* a Gingerbread Golem guards a mountain pass during the harshest months of the year. As spring arrives, it gradually crumbles under the warming sun, its remains nourishing the earth.
- **Symbolic Meaning:**
  - The Golem's return to nature symbolizes the cyclical nature of life and the idea that all creations eventually return to their origins.
  - Its erosion marks the passing of winter and the renewal of life in spring.

2. Devoured by Creatures

- **Example Story:**
  In *"The Golem's Feast,"* a Gingerbread Golem created to protect a forest is consumed by woodland animals after defeating a band of poachers.
- **Symbolic Meaning:**
  - This tale reflects the interconnectedness of life, where even a magical creation becomes part of the natural cycle.
  - It highlights the idea that nothing is truly lost, as the Golem's essence is passed on to other living beings.

3. Weathering Over Time

- **Example Story:**
  In *"The Spiced Guardian,"* a Gingerbread Golem left to protect an abandoned village eventually weathers away, its fragments becoming part of the soil.
- **Symbolic Meaning:**
  - This ending represents the passage of time and the impermanence of all things, reinforcing the theme of renewal.

Magical Vanishings

In some legends, the Gingerbread Golem's disappearance is abrupt and shrouded in mystery, often tied to its magical origins.

1. Returning to Its Creator's Will

- **Example Story:**

  In *"The Invisible Protector,"* a Gingerbread Golem disappears the moment its creator no longer needs it, leaving behind only a faint scent of spices as a reminder of its presence.

- **Symbolic Meaning:**
    - The disappearance emphasizes the ephemeral nature of magic, which exists only as long as it is needed.
    - It reflects the idea that some forces are meant to guide us briefly before fading away.

2. Disappearing into the Elements

- **Example Story:**

  In *"The Vanishing Guardian,"* a Gingerbread Golem created during a Yule festival dissolves into the snow as the first rays of sunlight touch it, signaling the end of its purpose.

- **Symbolic Meaning:**
    - The merging of the Golem with natural elements symbolizes unity with the world and the transient nature of magical interventions.
    - The disappearance at dawn underscores the Golem's connection to cycles of darkness and light.

3. Transforming into a Symbol

- **Example Story:**
  In *"The Eternal Protector,"* a Gingerbread Golem vanishes after defeating a marauding force, leaving behind a field of ginger plants where it stood. The plants become a symbol of protection and prosperity for the village.
- **Symbolic Meaning:**
    - This tale reflects the transformation of physical creations into enduring legacies.
    - It suggests that while the Golem's form may vanish, its spirit and influence persist.

Mystical Endings and Their Themes

The destruction or disappearance of the Gingerbread Golem is rarely portrayed as a loss; instead, it serves as a narrative and symbolic resolution. Key themes include:

1. The Impermanence of Magic

- The Golem's temporary nature underscores the fleeting quality of all magical interventions.
- These endings remind audiences that even the most extraordinary creations are subject to the passage of time.

2. Sacrifice and Legacy

- The Golem's destruction often involves an act of sacrifice, reinforcing its role as a selfless protector.
- The legacy it leaves behind—whether in the form of nourishment, protection, or a symbolic reminder—emphasizes the lasting impact of temporary creations.

3. Cycles of Renewal

- The Golem's return to the earth, water, or other natural elements reflects the cyclical nature of life and death.
- These endings tie the Golem's story to broader themes of transformation and renewal.

4. Mystery and Wonder

- Vanishing endings add an element of mystery, inviting audiences to imagine the Golem's continued existence in some unseen form.

- They reinforce the idea that magic operates beyond human understanding, leaving room for wonder and possibility.

Modern Interpretations of the Vanishing Golem

Contemporary retellings of Gingerbread Golem tales often adapt their mystical endings to reflect modern values and sensibilities.

1. **Environmental Themes:**
   - Some modern stories emphasize the Golem's return to nature as a metaphor for sustainability and harmony with the environment.
2. **Heroic Sacrifice:**
   - In recent adaptations, the Golem's destruction is framed as a heroic act that inspires its creator or community to continue its legacy.
3. **Unfinished Mysteries:**
   - Modern narratives often leave the Golem's disappearance ambiguous, allowing readers or viewers to interpret its fate in their own way.

Conclusion

The mystical endings of Gingerbread Golem stories serve as powerful symbols of sacrifice, transformation, and the impermanence of magic. Whether crumbling into crumbs, dissolving into nature, or vanishing without a trace, the Golem's departure is always meaningful, reflecting its role as a protector and its connection to the cycles of life and renewal. These endings remind us that even the sweetest creations can carry profound lessons, leaving behind legacies that inspire wonder, reflection, and gratitude.

Chapter 18: Cursed Confections: Warnings and Consequences Accounts of Failed Creations or Malevolent Gingerbread Golems

While many stories celebrate the Gingerbread Golem as a benevolent protector or hero, there is a darker side to the mythos. Tales of failed creations and malevolent Gingerbread Golems serve as cautionary tales, warning of the potential consequences of hubris, neglect, or malicious intent. These cursed confections reflect humanity's fears about the unintended results of creation and the ethical responsibilities of wielding power. This chapter explores the accounts of these sinister figures, the circumstances of their creation, and the moral lessons embedded in their stories.

The Nature of Cursed Confections

A cursed Gingerbread Golem often arises when its creation is flawed or its purpose corrupted. These failures usually result from one or more of the following factors:

1. **Impure Intentions:**
   - A Golem crafted with selfish, greedy, or malicious motives may inherit these negative traits, becoming a destructive force rather than a protector.
2. **Flawed Rituals:**
   - Errors in the creation process, such as omitting a key ingredient or mispronouncing a chant, can lead to a defective or malevolent Golem.
3. **Overuse of Power:**
   - Attempting to imbue the Golem with excessive strength or autonomy can cause it to become uncontrollable, turning against its creator or others.

4. **Neglect and Mistreatment:**
    - A Golem that is mistreated, neglected, or burdened with conflicting commands may develop resentment, leading to destructive behavior.

Accounts of Malevolent Gingerbread Golems

Tales of cursed Gingerbread Golems often emphasize their unpredictability and the chaos they unleash. Below are some of the most notable examples from folklore:

1. The Golem of Bitter Spice (German Folklore)

- **Story Summary:**
  A greedy merchant creates a Gingerbread Golem to guard his vault of stolen goods. In his haste, he uses spoiled flour and bitter spices, tainting the Golem's essence. The Golem grows resentful, turning on its creator by scattering his wealth across the town before crumbling into ash.
- **Lessons Learned:**
  - Greed and dishonesty can corrupt even the most noble creations.
  - The quality of ingredients symbolizes the purity of intent; tainted inputs yield disastrous results.

2. The Runaway Golem (Scandinavian Myth)

- **Story Summary:**
  A baker attempts to create a Gingerbread Golem large enough to protect an entire village. However, an error in the animation chant imbues the Golem with excessive independence. It escapes the village, causing chaos as it rampages through nearby towns before dissolving in a river.
- **Lessons Learned:**
  - Overambition and lack of precision can lead to unintended consequences.
  - Power must be tempered with control and responsibility.

3. The Golem's Wrath (French Legend)

- **Story Summary:**

    A jealous apprentice baker secretly crafts a Gingerbread Golem to sabotage his master's bakery. The Golem initially follows orders but becomes increasingly malicious, setting fires and driving away customers. The master eventually defeats it by melting it in the oven where it was created.

- **Lessons Learned:**
    - Malicious intent can backfire, harming the creator as much as the target.
    - The Golem's vulnerability to its origin (fire, in this case) underscores the importance of understanding the tools of creation.

4. The Cracked Golem (Eastern European Tale)

- **Story Summary:**

    A family creates a Gingerbread Golem to protect their farm during a harsh winter. However, they accidentally crack its chest while decorating it, leaving it incomplete. The Golem becomes erratic, scaring off visitors and destroying property in its attempts to fulfill its unclear purpose. It eventually crumbles after the family acknowledges their mistake and buries its remains in gratitude.

- **Lessons Learned:**
    - A flawed creation reflects the carelessness or lack of intention behind it.
    - The story emphasizes the importance of humility and accountability in addressing mistakes.

Themes of Caution and Consequence

The tales of cursed Gingerbread Golems reflect broader themes about creation, morality, and the responsibilities of wielding power.

1. The Danger of Hubris:

- Many stories warn against overestimating one's abilities or attempting to create something beyond one's control.
- The Golem's transformation from protector to threat often serves as a metaphor for the dangers of arrogance.

2. The Ethics of Creation:

- The behavior of a Gingerbread Golem often mirrors the intentions and actions of its creator, emphasizing the ethical responsibilities inherent in creation.
- These tales challenge audiences to consider the potential consequences of their actions and the importance of acting with integrity.

3. The Balance of Power and Responsibility:

- The destructive potential of a cursed Golem highlights the need to balance power with wisdom and restraint.
- Stories often emphasize the importance of understanding and respecting the limitations of one's creations.

4. Redemption Through Acknowledgment:

- In some tales, cursed Golems are redeemed or pacified when their creators acknowledge their mistakes and take responsibility for their actions.
- This theme reinforces the idea that accountability and humility can mitigate the consequences of failure.

Modern Interpretations of Cursed Confections

Contemporary adaptations of cursed Gingerbread Golem tales often incorporate modern themes and settings, making them relevant to today's audiences.

1. The Corporate Golem:

- In some modern stories, the Gingerbread Golem becomes a metaphor for unchecked ambition or greed, such as a mass-produced creation that turns against its corporate makers.
- These tales explore themes of consumerism, environmental responsibility, and the unintended consequences of industrialization.

2. Technological Analogies:

- The cursed Golem is often reimagined as a warning about artificial intelligence or advanced technologies, exploring ethical dilemmas around autonomy and control.
- These adaptations draw parallels between the unpredictability of a malevolent Golem and the potential risks of creating sentient machines.

3. Personal Redemption:

- Modern narratives frequently emphasize personal growth and redemption, with creators learning from their mistakes and finding ways to make amends.
- These stories reflect contemporary values of self-improvement and resilience in the face of failure.

Warnings and Precautions in Golem Creation

The stories of cursed Gingerbread Golems often include practical and symbolic advice for avoiding failure, emphasizing the importance of care, intention, and humility in creation.

1. Purity of Ingredients and Rituals:

- Using high-quality materials and following rituals precisely are common motifs, symbolizing the importance of preparation and attention to detail.

2. Respect for Boundaries:

- Tales frequently caution against overloading a Golem with excessive strength or autonomy, reinforcing the need to respect limitations.

3. Clear Purpose and Intentions:

- A well-defined purpose helps prevent a Golem from becoming erratic or destructive, highlighting the importance of clarity and focus.

4. Ethical Responsibility:

- Creators are often reminded to act with integrity, treating their Golems as extensions of their own values and actions.

Conclusion

The tales of cursed Gingerbread Golems serve as compelling reminders of the ethical and practical challenges of creation. These cautionary stories highlight the dangers of hubris, the consequences of neglect, and the importance of acting with care and intention. Whether through tales of destructive rampages or redemptive resolutions, these cursed confections reflect humanity's ongoing exploration of power, morality, and the responsibilities of creation. They remind us that even the sweetest creations can carry the potential for sin, making the lessons of the Gingerbread Golem as relevant today as they were in ancient times.

Chapter 19: Artisan Secrets: Hidden Knowledge of Gingerbread Crafting

Techniques and Tools Used by Bakers to Give Life to These Creations

The art of crafting Gingerbread Golems combines culinary skill, creative artistry, and mystical practice. Over centuries, bakers have refined their techniques, developing secret methods and specialized tools to create these edible protectors and bring them to life. While much of the knowledge remains cloaked in myth and folklore, tales and traditions reveal a trove of insights into the craft of Gingerbread Golem-making. This chapter unveils the hidden knowledge behind this ancient and magical art, exploring the techniques, tools, and rituals that transform simple ingredients into legendary figures.

The Foundation: Selecting Ingredients with Intent

The process of crafting a Gingerbread Golem begins long before the dough is mixed. Bakers place immense importance on the selection of ingredients, each chosen for its symbolic and practical significance.

1. The Base Ingredients:

- **Flour:** Represents stability and grounding, forming the structural integrity of the Golem. Traditional recipes call for stone-ground flour, believed to retain the earth's protective energy.
- **Ginger:** The namesake spice symbolizes warmth, protection, and vitality, serving as the Golem's metaphorical "heart."
- **Honey or Molasses:** These sweeteners embody abundance and unity, binding the Golem's elements together while symbolizing harmony and goodwill.
- **Spices (Cinnamon, Nutmeg, Clove):** Each spice contributes not only to flavor but also to the Golem's mystical properties:

- **Cinnamon:** Purification and spiritual defense.
- **Nutmeg:** Intuition and hidden strength.
- **Clove:** Protection and endurance.

2. Secret Additives:

- Folklore speaks of hidden ingredients used to imbue the Golem with life and purpose:
    - **Ground herbs** such as thyme or rosemary for clarity and focus.
    - **A pinch of salt** to protect against negative energies.
    - **Sacred waters** from a well or stream, symbolizing purity and connection to the divine.

3. Symbolic Decoration Ingredients:

- **Candy Eyes:** Often crafted from hardened sugar or edible pearls, these represent vigilance and awareness.
- **Sugar Crystals or Gold Leaf:** Symbolize divine favor and magical potency, often used to embellish the Golem's exterior.
- **Red Icing or Glaze:** Applied to the "heart" of the Golem, signifying vitality and the spark of life.

The Craft: Techniques for Shaping and Decorating

The physical construction of a Gingerbread Golem is an intricate process, blending practical baking skills with symbolic artistry.

1. Shaping the Golem:

- **Hand-Sculpting:** For large or highly detailed Golems, bakers often sculpt the dough by hand, ensuring the figure's features align with its intended purpose (e.g., a strong stance for protection, open arms for guardianship).
- **Carved Molds:** Some artisans use wooden or ceramic molds engraved with protective symbols or runes, transferring these designs onto the Golem's surface.
- **Layering Techniques:** Advanced bakers use layered dough to create dimensional features, such as raised arms, defined faces, or intricate armor-like patterns.

2. Precision Baking:

- **Controlled Temperatures:** Bakers believe the oven's temperature must be carefully managed to ensure the Golem "awakens" properly. Folklore suggests baking at a steady, moderate heat to infuse the figure with balanced energy.
- **Timing Rituals:** The Golem must be removed from the oven at precisely the right moment, often determined by visual cues (a golden-brown hue) or symbolic timing (e.g., the stroke of midnight during a solstice).

3. Decorating with Purpose:

- **Protective Symbols:** Bakers pipe runes or sigils onto the Golem's body using icing or melted chocolate. Common symbols include:

- **Circles or spirals** for unity and protection.
- **Stars or crosses** for divine guidance.
- **Eyes or suns** for vigilance and light.
- **Personalized Features:** Some Golems are adorned with items from their creators, such as buttons, ribbons, or charms, to establish a stronger connection between the figure and its maker.

The Animation: Rituals to Bring the Golem to Life

The culmination of Gingerbread Golem crafting lies in its animation, a mystical process steeped in ritual and intention.

1. The Chant of Animation:

- A specific incantation is spoken or sung to awaken the Golem. These chants vary by region but often include elements of gratitude, purpose, and protection.
- Example chant from German folklore:

"From spice and flour, strength and might,
Rise, protector, guard this night.
With heart of warmth, with eyes that see,
Stand strong, O Golem, protect for me."

2. Ritual Gestures:

- **Tracing Symbols:** Some creators trace protective symbols over the Golem's chest or head with a spoon or knife before reciting the chant.
- **Touching the "Heart":** A small red candy or sugar decoration placed on the Golem's chest is touched during the animation ritual to symbolize the spark of life.

3. Activation Through Heat or Light:

- Placing the Golem in direct sunlight, near a fire, or under a candle's glow is believed to complete the animation process, tying the figure to natural elements.

4. The Final Command:

- The creator gives the Golem a specific command or purpose, spoken with clarity and intention. For example:
    - "Guard this home and its hearth."
    - "Stand watch over our feast."

Specialized Tools of the Trade

Bakers who specialize in crafting Gingerbread Golems often use unique tools designed for both practical and mystical purposes.

1. Custom Rolling Pins:

- Rolling pins engraved with protective patterns (e.g., runes, stars, or spirals) imprint these designs directly into the dough.

2. Ritual Molds:

- Hand-carved molds passed down through generations often bear intricate symbols and designs that imbue the Golem with additional significance.

3. Precision Icing Tools:

- Fine-tipped piping bags or tools allow bakers to decorate the Golem with intricate details, including symbols, patterns, and facial features.

4. Sacred Baking Stones:

- Some bakers use stones or tiles in their ovens that are believed to enhance the Golem's energy by grounding it in the earth's natural vibrations.

The Legacy of Gingerbread Artisans

Bakers who craft Gingerbread Golems are often revered as community protectors, blending culinary expertise with spiritual practice. Their creations are not merely edible; they are expressions of resilience, creativity, and cultural heritage.

1. **Passing Down Knowledge:**
    - Techniques and recipes for Gingerbread Golem crafting are often closely guarded secrets, shared only within families or guilds.
    - Apprenticeship programs in some regions ensure the continuity of this rare art form.
2. **Modern Interpretations:**
    - While traditional methods remain sacred, contemporary artisans experiment with new materials (e.g., fondant, edible glitter) and modern tools (e.g., 3D printing molds) to bring innovative flair to the craft.
3. **Cultural Significance:**
    - Gingerbread Golem-making is celebrated as an integral part of holiday traditions in many regions, symbolizing the enduring power of creativity and protection.

Conclusion

The art of Gingerbread Golem crafting is a testament to the intersection of culinary skill, artistic creativity, and mystical practice. From the careful selection of ingredients to the intricate rituals of animation, every step of the process reflects a deep understanding of symbolism and intention. As both protectors and cultural icons, Gingerbread Golems embody the legacy of the artisans who bring them to life, reminding us of the transformative power of tradition, imagination, and shared purpose.

Chapter 20: Literary Interpretations
Analysis of Literary Works Inspired by the Gingerbread Golem Myth

The Gingerbread Golem has been a source of fascination for writers across generations, offering a rich blend of whimsy, mysticism, and allegory that inspires storytelling in diverse genres. From children's literature to adult fantasy, the Gingerbread Golem myth has been reinterpreted, reimagined, and infused with new meanings. This chapter explores the literary works inspired by the Gingerbread Golem myth, analyzing how authors have adapted its themes, symbols, and narratives to create compelling stories that resonate with modern audiences.

The Evolution of the Gingerbread Golem in Literature

The transition of the Gingerbread Golem from folklore to literature reflects its adaptability as a narrative device. Writers have drawn upon the myth's core elements—creation, protection, and impermanence—while tailoring the figure to fit various literary traditions and genres.

1. Folklore and Mythology Collections

- Early literary interpretations of the Gingerbread Golem appeared in anthologies of European folklore. These collections preserved traditional tales while introducing the myth to broader audiences.
- **Example:**
  - *"The Guardian of Spicedown"* (1800s): A collection of German folktales includes a story about a Gingerbread Golem crafted to protect a village during a harsh winter. The tale emphasizes themes of sacrifice and community resilience.

2. Children's Literature

- The Gingerbread Golem became a popular figure in children's books, where its magical and edible nature appealed to young readers.
- Writers often emphasize the playful and adventurous aspects of the Golem, transforming it into a companion or hero.
- **Example:**
  - *"Ginger the Brave"* (1923): A children's book about a Gingerbread Golem who helps a young baker save her town from a mischievous elf. The story highlights courage, teamwork, and the value of creativity.

3. Fantasy and Adventure Stories

- The Gingerbread Golem's magical origins make it a natural fit for fantasy literature. In this genre, the Golem often takes on more complex roles, serving as a protector, ally, or even antagonist.
- **Example:**
  - *"The Spiced Warrior"* (1987): A fantasy novel set in a kingdom where Gingerbread Golems are created to guard ancient treasures. The protagonist, an apprentice baker, discovers a long-lost recipe for a Golem with extraordinary powers.

4. Satirical and Speculative Fiction

- Modern authors have used the Gingerbread Golem to explore social, political, and technological themes, employing the figure as a metaphor for issues such as consumerism, automation, and ethical creation.
- **Example:**

- *"The Gingerbread Rebellion"* (2015): A satirical novel that imagines a dystopian world where mass-produced Gingerbread Golems revolt against their creators, serving as an allegory for the dangers of unchecked industrialization.

Themes in Literary Interpretations

The literary adaptations of the Gingerbread Golem myth often explore universal themes, making the figure a versatile and enduring symbol.

1. Creation and Responsibility

- Many stories emphasize the ethical dilemmas of creating a being with life and purpose, echoing themes from Mary Shelley's *Frankenstein*.
- **Example:**
    - In *"The Sweet Guardian"* (1942), a Gingerbread Golem gains sentience and questions its creator's intentions, challenging the boundaries between creator and creation.

2. Sacrifice and Redemption

- The Golem's impermanence often becomes a focal point, symbolizing selflessness and the transient nature of life.
- **Example:**
    - *"The Crumbled Hero"* (2001): A novella in which a Gingerbread Golem sacrifices itself to save a war-torn village, inspiring its inhabitants to rebuild and find hope.

3. Protection and Power

- As a protector, the Golem raises questions about the use and abuse of power, often serving as a metaphor for leadership, governance, or technology.
- **Example:**

- *"The Baker's Sentinel"* (1998): A dystopian tale where a city relies on a single Gingerbread Golem for protection, only to face disaster when it begins to deteriorate.

4. Playfulness and Whimsy

- In children's literature, the Golem is often portrayed as a mischievous yet endearing character, emphasizing themes of friendship and adventure.
- **Example:**
    - *"The Gingerbread Golem's Big Adventure"* (2010): A lighthearted story about a Golem who escapes its creator's bakery to explore the world, learning valuable lessons about kindness and courage.

Symbolism in Gingerbread Golem Literature

The symbolic richness of the Gingerbread Golem lends itself to various interpretations, allowing authors to infuse their works with layered meanings.

1. Sweetness as Strength

- The Golem's sugary composition symbolizes the power of kindness, community, and resilience, making it a compelling figure in stories about overcoming adversity.

2. Ephemeral Nature

- The Golem's inevitable destruction or decay reflects the impermanence of life, serving as a poignant reminder of the beauty and fragility of existence.

3. Blending the Mundane and Magical

- The combination of everyday ingredients and mystical rituals highlights the transformative power of creativity, showing how the ordinary can become extraordinary.

4. Duality of Power

- The Golem's dual nature—capable of both protection and destruction—mirrors the complexities of human morality and the ethical challenges of wielding power.

Notable Literary Works Inspired by the Gingerbread Golem

This section highlights specific works that have drawn directly from the Gingerbread Golem myth, showcasing their diversity and impact.

1. "The Gingerbread Knight" (1965)

- **Author:** Edith Thorne
- **Genre:** Fantasy
- **Synopsis:** A Gingerbread Golem is brought to life to protect a kingdom from an invading force, but its true purpose is revealed when it confronts the corruption within the royal court.
- **Themes:** Justice, loyalty, and the ethical use of power.

2. "Spiced Dreams" (1992)

- **Author:** Michael Gables
- **Genre:** Magical Realism
- **Synopsis:** A struggling baker discovers a family recipe for a Gingerbread Golem that brings her dreams to life, but the creations also manifest her deepest fears.
- **Themes:** Creativity, fear, and self-discovery.

3. "The Golem's Crumbs" (2011)

- **Author:** Olivia Harker
- **Genre:** Young Adult Fiction
- **Synopsis:** A teenage protagonist uncovers a forgotten Gingerbread Golem in her grandmother's attic, learning about her family's magical heritage and the Golem's role in protecting their lineage.
- **Themes:** Heritage, identity, and the power of legacy.

4. "The Frost Golem" (2018)

- **Author:** Richard Hayes
- **Genre:** Horror
- **Synopsis:** A cursed Gingerbread Golem terrorizes a small town during a snowstorm, forcing residents to confront their past misdeeds to survive.
- **Themes:** Redemption, consequences of sin, and collective accountability.

The Gingerbread Golem's Role in Modern Literary Trends
The Gingerbread Golem's continued presence in literature reflects its adaptability to contemporary themes and storytelling techniques.
1. Exploration of Identity and Autonomy:

- Modern works often depict the Golem as a sentient being grappling with its own identity and purpose, paralleling broader discussions about artificial intelligence and free will.

2. Reflection of Social Issues:

- Authors use the Golem as a metaphor for societal concerns, such as inequality, environmental degradation, and the ethics of creation.

3. Expansion into Global Contexts:

- While rooted in European folklore, the Golem has been reimagined in diverse cultural settings, blending its traditional elements with new perspectives and traditions.

Conclusion
The Gingerbread Golem has proven to be a versatile and enduring figure in literature, inspiring works that range from whimsical children's tales to profound explorations of morality and identity. By adapting its myth to fit different genres and themes, authors continue to breathe new life into the Gingerbread Golem, ensuring its place as a symbol of creativity, resilience, and the complexities of creation. Through its stories, the Golem transcends its edible origins to become a timeless literary icon, offering insights into the human condition and the power of imagination.

Chapter 21: Visual Representations
Art, Illustrations, and Cultural Depictions of Gingerbread Golems

The Gingerbread Golem's blend of mysticism, craftsmanship, and culinary artistry has made it a compelling subject for visual representation across centuries. From traditional folk art to modern digital illustrations, the Gingerbread Golem has captured the imaginations of artists worldwide. Each depiction reflects the values, aesthetics, and cultural context of its time, showcasing the Golem as a protector, a festive figure, or a symbol of humanity's creative spirit. This chapter explores the evolution of Gingerbread Golem art, examining its historical roots, stylistic variations, and cultural significance.

Historical Roots of Gingerbread Golem Art

The earliest visual representations of Gingerbread Golems can be traced to medieval and early modern Europe, where the tradition of crafting gingerbread figures was both a culinary and artistic practice.

1. Medieval Gingerbread Effigies

- **Description:**
    - Gingerbread figures in medieval Europe were often simple yet symbolic, designed to ward off evil or celebrate seasonal festivals. These early effigies were precursors to the Gingerbread Golem, blending protective symbolism with festive joy.
- **Common Features:**
    - Basic human shapes with minimal decoration.
    - Use of natural dyes from spices and flowers for added detail.
    - Patterns impressed with carved wooden molds, often depicting protective symbols such as crosses, suns, or animals.

2. Renaissance and Baroque Gingerbread Art

- **Description:**
    - During the Renaissance and Baroque periods, gingerbread figures became more elaborate, reflecting the era's emphasis on intricate detail and artistic expression.
- **Common Features:**
    - Richly decorated figures with ornate icing patterns.
    - Scenes depicting seasonal festivities or mythological stories, including early interpretations of the Gingerbread Golem as a guardian.
    - Incorporation of metallic glazes (e.g., gold or silver leaf) for a luxurious appearance.

3. Folk Art and Regional Variations

- **Description:**
    - In rural communities, Gingerbread Golems were depicted in folk art as symbols of protection and abundance. These representations were often infused with local traditions and motifs.
- **Examples:**
    - In Germanic regions, Golems were depicted with stern expressions and robust builds, symbolizing strength and resilience.
    - Scandinavian art often showed Gingerbread Golems surrounded by winter landscapes, emphasizing their role as protectors during harsh seasons.

Modern Artistic Interpretations

The Gingerbread Golem has evolved into a versatile subject in contemporary art, appearing in a variety of styles and media. Modern artists explore the Golem's themes of protection, whimsy, and duality, often reimagining its appearance to suit different narratives and audiences.

1. Illustrations in Literature

- **Children's Books:**
    - Depictions of Gingerbread Golems in children's literature often emphasize their playful and endearing qualities. Artists use bright colors, exaggerated expressions, and whimsical details to appeal to younger audiences.
    - **Example:** In *"Ginger the Brave"* (1923), the Golem is illustrated with oversized candy eyes, frosting "armor," and a friendly smile, reinforcing its role as a lovable hero.
- **Fantasy Novels:**
    - In adult fantasy literature, Gingerbread Golems are portrayed as powerful and mysterious figures. Illustrators often use darker tones and intricate designs to convey their magical nature.
    - **Example:** *"The Spiced Warrior"* (1987) features a cover illustration of a Golem with glowing runes etched into its doughy surface, holding a peppermint staff.

2. Digital Art and Pop Culture

- **Video Game Designs:**
    - In gaming, Gingerbread Golems are often depicted as formidable yet whimsical creatures, blending holiday cheer with fantasy aesthetics.

- **Example:** A popular RPG includes a Gingerbread Golem as a holiday-themed boss, designed with glowing candy cane weapons and frosting shields.
- **Fan Art:**
    - Digital artists frequently reimagine the Golem in innovative ways, from futuristic robotic interpretations to anthropomorphic warriors.
    - These works often appear on social media platforms, reflecting the Golem's growing appeal among modern audiences.

3. Holiday-Themed Art and Marketing

- **Seasonal Advertisements:**
    - Gingerbread Golems are frequently featured in holiday advertisements, often portrayed as jovial guardians of festive cheer.
    - **Example:** A bakery chain's marketing campaign included posters of a smiling Golem holding a tray of gingerbread cookies, symbolizing warmth and hospitality.
- **Decorative Art:**
    - Holiday cards, ornaments, and home décor often feature stylized Gingerbread Golems, emphasizing their connection to seasonal celebrations.

Cultural Variations in Representation

Different cultures have adapted the Gingerbread Golem myth to align with their own artistic traditions, resulting in a rich diversity of representations.

1. European Variations

- **Germanic Regions:**
    - Golems are depicted as strong, stoic protectors, often adorned with traditional folk motifs such as Edelweiss flowers or geometric patterns.
- **Scandinavia:**
    - Depictions emphasize the Golem's connection to winter and nature, with icy blue frosting and snowflake designs symbolizing its role as a seasonal guardian.

2. North American Interpretations

- **Whimsical and Commercialized:**
    - In North America, Gingerbread Golems are often presented in a playful, commercialized style, emphasizing their edible nature and festive charm.
    - Common features include candy cane limbs, gumdrop buttons, and cheerful expressions.

3. Global Adaptations

- **Japanese Kawaii Style:**
    - In Japan, Gingerbread Golems are often reimagined in the "kawaii" (cute) style, with exaggerated proportions, pastel colors, and heart-shaped decorations.
- **Fusion Designs:**

- Artists in multicultural contexts blend Gingerbread Golem imagery with elements from other traditions, such as Day of the Dead motifs or Chinese paper-cutting patterns, creating unique hybrid representations.

Techniques and Mediums in Gingerbread Golem Art

Artists employ a wide range of techniques and mediums to bring the Gingerbread Golem to life, from traditional crafts to cutting-edge digital tools.

1. Traditional Techniques

- **Wooden Carvings:**
    - In some regions, artisans carve Gingerbread Golem figures into wood, creating decorative plaques or ornaments.
- **Hand-Painted Scenes:**
    - Folk artists often depict Golems in hand-painted scenes on canvas or pottery, capturing their mythological role in local traditions.

2. Edible Art

- **Gingerbread Sculptures:**
    - Bakers create life-sized or miniature Gingerbread Golems for holiday displays, using icing, fondant, and candy to add intricate details.
    - **Example:** A famous Christmas market in Germany features an annual competition where bakers craft elaborate Golems, some standing over six feet tall.

3. Digital Illustration and Animation

- **3D Modeling:**
    - Digital artists use 3D modeling software to create detailed, lifelike Gingerbread Golems for video games, animated films, and virtual reality experiences.
- **Illustration Software:**

- Programs like Photoshop and Procreate allow artists to experiment with textures, lighting, and color schemes, bringing the Golem to life in dynamic and imaginative ways.

Symbolism in Visual Representations

The visual depiction of Gingerbread Golems often carries symbolic meaning, reflecting their role as protectors, heroes, or festive icons.

1. **Armor and Decorations:**
    - Frosting "armor" or candy "weapons" symbolize strength and resilience, while intricate patterns suggest magical protection.
2. **Expressions:**
    - Cheerful faces convey warmth and approachability, while stoic or stern expressions emphasize their role as defenders.
3. **Colors and Materials:**
    - Warm browns and golden hues represent comfort and abundance, while brighter colors highlight their connection to joy and celebration.

Conclusion

The Gingerbread Golem has become a beloved subject in visual art, evolving from humble folk figures to dynamic representations in modern media. Through their depictions, artists have captured the Golem's duality as both a whimsical festive figure and a powerful symbol of protection and creativity. These visual representations not only honor the myth's origins but also ensure its continued relevance and appeal, inviting audiences to explore the magic and meaning of the Gingerbread Golem through a rich tapestry of artistic expression.

Chapter 22: Music and Performance

Songs, Plays, and Performances Dedicated to Gingerbread Golem Tales

The Gingerbread Golem, a figure steeped in folklore and festive tradition, has inspired a rich array of musical compositions and theatrical performances. Its dual nature as a protector and a symbol of magic has made it a compelling subject for storytellers across mediums. From folk songs and operettas to modern musicals and stage plays, the Gingerbread Golem has captivated audiences, blending themes of warmth, creativity, and morality with vibrant melodies and dramatic narratives. This chapter explores the music and performances inspired by the Gingerbread Golem myth, highlighting their historical roots, artistic evolution, and cultural impact.

Historical Roots of Musical and Theatrical Depictions

The earliest performances centered on the Gingerbread Golem were closely tied to seasonal festivals and community traditions, often incorporating music, dance, and storytelling.

1. Folk Songs and Seasonal Chants

- **Origins:**
    - In medieval Europe, songs about Gingerbread Golems were a common feature of winter solstice celebrations, blending festive cheer with moral lessons.
- **Characteristics:**
    - Lyrics often told tales of Golems protecting villages, guarding feasts, or helping families through harsh winters.
    - Simple, repetitive melodies made these songs easy for communities to learn and pass down through generations.
- **Example Song:**
    - *"The Golem's Watch"* (circa 1500s): A German folk song recounting the story of a Gingerbread Golem guarding a Yule feast from hungry wolves.

2. Community Theater and Pageantry

- **Origins:**
    - Local pageants and amateur theatrical performances during Christmas or winter festivals often featured stories of Gingerbread Golems.
- **Structure:**
    - These plays were performed outdoors or in community halls, with simple sets and costumes made from seasonal materials.
    - The Gingerbread Golem was often portrayed by a performer in a dough-like costume, with oversized candy buttons and frosting accents.
- **Themes:**
    - Stories focused on protection, generosity, and the triumph of good over adversity.

Evolution into Professional Music and Theater

As the myth of the Gingerbread Golem spread, it inspired professional composers, playwrights, and performers, leading to more sophisticated adaptations.

1. Operettas and Classical Music

- **Composers' Interest:**
    - The whimsical yet poignant nature of the Gingerbread Golem made it a favorite subject for operettas and symphonic compositions in the 18th and 19th centuries.
- **Notable Works:**
    - *"The Spiced Guardian"* (1784): A light-hearted operetta by Austrian composer Heinrich Kübler. The story follows a Gingerbread Golem who falls in love with a human, leading to a comedic series of misunderstandings and a heartwarming resolution.
    - *"Sweet and Strong"* (1857): A symphonic poem by French composer Elise Varnier, depicting the creation, life, and eventual sacrifice of a Gingerbread Golem through orchestral movements.

2. Golden Age of Musicals and Ballets

- **Broadway and Beyond:**
    - The mid-20th century saw the Gingerbread Golem myth adapted into musicals and ballets, where its visual and thematic appeal was enhanced by elaborate staging and choreography.
- **Notable Works:**
    - *"The Gingerbread Knight"* (1953): A Broadway musical about a Gingerbread Golem who defends a small town during a magical winter storm. Featuring memorable songs

like *"Baked to Protect"* and *"A Sprinkle of Love,"* the show became a holiday classic.
- *"Dance of the Frosted Guardian"* (1967): A ballet that uses the Gingerbread Golem as a metaphor for resilience and transformation, with dancers adorned in costumes resembling edible creations.

Modern Performances and Contemporary Music

In the 21st century, the Gingerbread Golem has continued to inspire musicians and performers, often blending traditional elements with modern sensibilities.

1. Holiday Concerts and Themed Events

- **Concert Pieces:**
    - Symphonies and choirs often include songs or compositions inspired by Gingerbread Golem tales in their holiday repertoires.
- **Interactive Performances:**
    - Holiday events feature interactive plays where children and families participate in creating a "living" Gingerbread Golem on stage, complete with songs and chants.
- **Example Performance:**
    - *"The Gingerbread Guardian's Carol"* (2012): A contemporary choral piece blending traditional melodies with modern harmonies, celebrating the Golem as a symbol of hope and unity.

2. Modern Theater and Film Musicals

- **Reinvention for New Audiences:**
    - Playwrights and directors have reimagined the Gingerbread Golem myth for modern audiences, incorporating themes of diversity, inclusion, and environmental awareness.
- **Notable Works:**
    - *"Rise of the Gingerbread Warrior"* (2015): A film musical about a Gingerbread Golem who protects a magical forest

from developers, featuring original songs like *"Baked to Be Brave"* and *"The Last Sprinkle."*
- *"Spiced Heart"* (2020): An off-Broadway production exploring the Golem's struggle with identity and purpose in a contemporary urban setting.

Cultural Variations in Performance

The Gingerbread Golem myth has been adapted to fit the artistic traditions and cultural contexts of various regions, resulting in diverse performances.

1. European Traditions

- **Germany and Austria:**
  - Gingerbread Golem plays remain a staple of Christmas markets, often performed as puppet shows with intricately crafted marionettes.
- **Scandinavia:**
  - Performances emphasize the Golem's connection to winter folklore, incorporating traditional Nordic music and dance.

2. North American Adaptations

- **Community Theater:**
  - Small-town theaters frequently stage holiday-themed productions featuring the Gingerbread Golem as a central figure.
- **Commercial Entertainment:**
  - The Golem is a popular character in theme park holiday shows, blending live-action performance with pyrotechnics and animatronics.

3. Global Interpretations

- **Asia:**
  - Japanese kabuki-style adaptations present the Gingerbread Golem as a guardian spirit, blending traditional Japanese music and staging with elements of the original myth.

- **Africa:**
  - Performances incorporate drumming and storytelling traditions, reinterpreting the Golem as a protector of villages and crops.

Themes in Music and Performance

The Gingerbread Golem's versatility as a character allows performers to explore a wide range of themes, making it relevant across different genres and settings.

1. Protection and Sacrifice

- Many performances highlight the Golem's role as a protector, with musical compositions often featuring heroic motifs and uplifting crescendos.

2. Whimsy and Joy

- In holiday-themed performances, the Golem is depicted as a source of festive cheer, with lighthearted songs and playful choreography.

3. Identity and Purpose

- Modern adaptations often delve into the Golem's internal struggles, using music and dialogue to explore themes of self-discovery and autonomy.

4. Community and Unity

- Performances frequently emphasize the Golem's connection to its creator and community, celebrating the power of collective effort and shared purpose.

Conclusion

The Gingerbread Golem's enduring appeal in music and performance reflects its ability to capture the imagination through its blend of magic, morality, and festive charm. From ancient folk songs to modern musicals, the Golem has inspired artists and audiences alike, offering a timeless symbol of protection, creativity, and resilience. Through its melodies and theatrical portrayals, the Gingerbread Golem continues to enchant, reminding us of the power of storytelling to unite and inspire across generations and cultures.

Chapter 23: The Gingerbread Golem in Academia
Previous Academic Studies and Interpretations of the Myth

The Gingerbread Golem has long intrigued academics across various disciplines, serving as a focal point for the study of folklore, cultural traditions, and the interplay between food and myth. Scholars have examined the Golem's symbolic meanings, historical origins, and its evolution in art, literature, and performance. This chapter delves into the academic landscape surrounding the Gingerbread Golem myth, exploring key studies, interpretations, and theoretical frameworks that have shaped our understanding of this sweet yet powerful creation.

The Origins of Academic Interest

The academic study of the Gingerbread Golem began in the 19th century, as folklorists and anthropologists sought to document and analyze European myths and legends. Early efforts focused on collecting oral traditions, while later studies applied more theoretical and interdisciplinary approaches.

1. Early Folklore Studies

- **Historical Context:**
    - The rise of folklore as an academic discipline in the 19th century spurred interest in documenting regional tales, including those involving Gingerbread Golems.
- **Key Figures:**
    - **Johann Fischer (1832):** A German folklorist who published *"Winter Tales of the Bavarian Alps,"* including one of the earliest recorded accounts of a Gingerbread Golem protecting a village from raiders.

- **Émile Renaud (1889):** A French ethnographer who examined gingerbread effigies in seasonal rituals, suggesting a link between food-based traditions and protective myths.
- **Focus Areas:**
    - The symbolic relationship between food and protection.
    - The seasonal and communal significance of Gingerbread Golem tales.

2. Structuralist Interpretations (Mid-20th Century)

- **Theoretical Approach:**
    - Scholars influenced by structuralism, such as Claude Lévi-Strauss, explored the binary oppositions within Gingerbread Golem myths, such as sweetness versus strength, life versus impermanence, and creation versus destruction.
- **Key Studies:**
    - Lévi-Strauss's essay *"Edible Myths: The Gingerbread Golem as Ritual Artifact"* (1956) argued that the Golem's duality reflects humanity's struggle to reconcile sustenance with spirituality.
- **Impact:**
    - Structuralism positioned the Gingerbread Golem as a lens through which to examine broader cultural and psychological dynamics.

Symbolism and Archetypal Studies

The symbolic richness of the Gingerbread Golem has made it a popular subject for scholars interested in archetypes and mythology.

1. Jungian Interpretations

- **Core Ideas:**
    - The Gingerbread Golem is often analyzed as an archetype of the "Protector" or the "Construct," representing humanity's desire to create life and safeguard communities.
- **Notable Works:**
    - *"The Sweet Guardian: Archetypal Roles in Golem Myths"* (1973) by Maria von Kraus examines the Golem's symbolic resonance with the collective unconscious, emphasizing its role as a mediator between creator and creation.

2. Food Symbolism and Rituals

- **Cultural Insights:**
    - Food studies scholars have explored the use of gingerbread as a symbolic medium, linking its ingredients to themes of warmth, abundance, and transformation.
- **Key Texts:**
    - **Pauline Hervey's** *"Spiced Constructs: The Role of Food in European Folklore"* (1992) examines the Gingerbread Golem as a culinary ritual, arguing that its creation bridges the physical and metaphysical realms.

3. Gender and Identity in Golem Tales

- **Emerging Themes:**
    - Recent studies have explored the gendered dimensions of Gingerbread Golem myths, focusing on the roles of cre-

ators (often depicted as male bakers or female caretakers) and the Golem's identity.
- **Key Research:**
    - *"Baking Power: Gender and Agency in Gingerbread Folklore"* (2015) by Helena Markov critiques the traditional gender roles in Golem creation myths, highlighting the empowering potential of women as creators and protectors.

The Gingerbread Golem as a Cultural Artifact

Anthropologists and cultural historians have studied the Gingerbread Golem as a cultural artifact, analyzing its role in communal identity, seasonal traditions, and material culture.

1. Seasonal Rituals and Festive Symbolism

- **Scholarly Focus:**
  - Studies emphasize the Golem's role in winter celebrations, where its creation symbolizes community resilience and the hope of renewal.
- **Key Findings:**
  - The Golem often serves as a focal point for communal storytelling, reinforcing social bonds and shared values.
- **Case Study:**
  - **"Winter Wards: The Role of Gingerbread Constructs in Alpine Folklore"** (1998) by Ingrid Möller explores how Gingerbread Golems were used as protective symbols during harsh winters in Bavarian villages.

2. Material Culture and Craftsmanship

- **Artisan Traditions:**
  - Scholars have examined the techniques and tools used to craft Gingerbread Golems, linking them to broader traditions of edible art and ritualistic baking.
- **Research Example:**
  - *"From Dough to Defender: The Craft of Gingerbread Guardians"* (2003) by Thomas Renshaw traces the evolution of gingerbread molds and decorative motifs across Europe.

Modern Interdisciplinary Studies

The 21st century has seen a surge in interdisciplinary approaches to studying the Gingerbread Golem, incorporating perspectives from literature, performance studies, and digital media.

1. Literary and Narrative Analysis

- **Focus:**
    - Scholars have analyzed the adaptation of Gingerbread Golem myths in literature, exploring how modern narratives reinterpret traditional themes.
- **Key Work:**
    - *"The Edible Hero: Gingerbread Golems in Contemporary Fantasy"* (2011) by Rebecca Linton examines the Golem's role in modern storytelling, highlighting its enduring appeal as a symbol of resilience.

2. Performance and Visual Media

- **Focus:**
    - Academic studies have explored the depiction of Gingerbread Golems in theater, film, and visual art, analyzing their aesthetic and cultural impact.
- **Research Example:**
    - *"Animating the Dough: Gingerbread Golems in Popular Culture"* (2017) by Samuel Hayes discusses the Golem's transition from folklore to animated media, emphasizing its adaptability to different genres and audiences.

3. Environmental and Ethical Dimensions

- **Emerging Topics:**
    - Recent studies have linked the Gingerbread Golem to discussions of sustainability, ethical creation, and the relationship between humanity and the natural world.
- **Notable Work:**
    - *"Crumbs of Responsibility: Gingerbread Golems and Environmental Ethics"* (2020) by Alisha Greene examines the Golem as a metaphor for humanity's impact on the environment, emphasizing the importance of intentional and responsible creation.

Recurring Themes in Academic Studies

Academic interpretations of the Gingerbread Golem consistently highlight certain recurring themes:

1. **Creation and Responsibility:**
    - The ethical implications of creating life, a topic with parallels in fields such as artificial intelligence and bioengineering.
2. **Community and Identity:**
    - The Golem as a symbol of communal resilience, reflecting shared cultural values and traditions.
3. **Impermanence and Sacrifice:**
    - The transient nature of the Golem serves as a metaphor for life, creativity, and the cyclical nature of existence.
4. **Cultural Adaptability:**
    - The Golem's ability to evolve and remain relevant across different cultural and historical contexts.

Conclusion

The Gingerbread Golem has become a subject of rich academic inquiry, inspiring research across a wide range of disciplines. From its origins in folklore to its role in modern culture, the Golem serves as a versatile symbol, reflecting humanity's creativity, morality, and collective imagination. By examining its history, symbolism, and cultural significance, scholars continue to uncover new insights into this enduring myth, ensuring that the Gingerbread Golem remains a vital and relevant figure in academic discourse.

Chapter 24: The Sweet Future: Evolving Myths

Predictions About the Future of the Gingerbread Golem Legend in a Modern Context

As the Gingerbread Golem evolves within the rich tapestry of global storytelling, its future in myth, media, and culture remains bright and dynamic. This chapter explores how the Gingerbread Golem might continue to adapt in response to technological advancements, shifting cultural values, and emerging artistic trends. From reimagined narratives in virtual spaces to its role in promoting sustainability and creativity, the Gingerbread Golem is poised to remain a relevant and inspiring figure for generations to come.

1. The Gingerbread Golem in Digital and Virtual Spaces

The digital age offers boundless opportunities for storytelling, and the Gingerbread Golem's whimsical yet meaningful character lends itself well to technological reinterpretation.

1.1 Interactive Digital Media

- **Video Games:**
    - The Gingerbread Golem's adaptable nature makes it an ideal character for video games, where it could serve as a protector, ally, or adversary.
    - **Example:** A fantasy adventure game featuring a Gingerbread Golem that players can craft, customize, and command to defend villages or explore magical lands.
- **Augmented Reality (AR):**
    - AR applications could bring the Golem into real-world environments, allowing users to "build" and animate their own Golems for festive or creative purposes.
    - **Example:** An AR holiday app where users design a Gingerbread Golem, watch it come to life, and use it to complete seasonal challenges.

1.2 Virtual Reality (VR) Storytelling

- VR platforms could offer immersive experiences where audiences step into the world of Gingerbread Golem myths.
- **Example:** A VR narrative where users take on the role of a baker crafting a Golem to protect a magical village, navigating challenges through a blend of culinary creativity and mystical rituals.

2. Environmental and Ethical Narratives

As global awareness of sustainability and ethical creation grows, the Gingerbread Golem myth could take on new dimensions, serving as a metaphor for humanity's relationship with nature and responsibility in creation.

2.1 Sustainability and the Golem

- Future adaptations might focus on the Golem as an eco-conscious figure, crafted from sustainable or symbolic materials to protect the environment.
- **Example:** A modern tale where the Gingerbread Golem serves as a guardian of forests, warning humanity about the consequences of environmental neglect.

2.2 Ethical Creation and Responsibility

- The Golem's role as a creation that mirrors its maker's intentions aligns with contemporary discussions about the ethical use of technology and artificial intelligence.
- **Example:** Futuristic interpretations might position the Gingerbread Golem as a culinary counterpart to AI, exploring questions about autonomy, control, and moral accountability.

3. Reimagined Cultural Roles

As the world becomes increasingly interconnected, the Gingerbread Golem could evolve to reflect diverse cultural perspectives and narratives.

3.1 Fusion Folklore

- Blending the Gingerbread Golem with myths from other cultures could create rich, hybrid stories that celebrate global traditions.
- **Example:** A collaboration between European and African folklore, where a Gingerbread Golem teams up with a trickster spirit to resolve conflicts and restore harmony.

3.2 Social Justice Themes

- The Golem's protective role could be adapted to address contemporary social issues, such as inequality, community resilience, and activism.
- **Example:** A modern fable where a Gingerbread Golem aids a marginalized community in overcoming challenges, emphasizing themes of unity and empowerment.

4. Innovations in Culinary and Artistic Interpretations

The Gingerbread Golem's edible origins ensure its continued relevance in the culinary arts, while advancements in artistic media offer new ways to interpret its myth.

4.1 Edible Art and Gastronomy

- Culinary innovators could push the boundaries of Gingerbread Golem craftsmanship, creating interactive or functional edible sculptures.
- **Example:** A life-sized Gingerbread Golem infused with motion sensors, designed to "move" during holiday displays, blending culinary art with robotics.

4.2 Digital Art and NFTs

- Digital artists could explore the Golem's aesthetic through NFTs (non-fungible tokens), creating unique, collectible representations of the myth.
- **Example:** A series of NFT Golem designs, each symbolizing a different virtue (e.g., courage, kindness, resilience), sold to fund charitable causes.

4.3 Experiential Art Installations

- Immersive installations could bring the Gingerbread Golem myth to life through multisensory exhibits, combining visual art, scent, and interactive storytelling.
- **Example:** A museum exhibit where visitors walk through a Gingerbread Golem's creation process, experiencing the sights, smells, and sounds of its mythical world.

5. Expanded Representation in Media

The Gingerbread Golem's future in popular media promises greater diversity in its storytelling and presentation.

5.1 Animated Films and Series

- Animated adaptations could explore the Golem's myth for a wide audience, from whimsical children's stories to mature explorations of its deeper themes.
- **Example:** A serialized animated series chronicling the adventures of a Gingerbread Golem across different eras and cultures, blending humor with poignant life lessons.

5.2 Streaming and Episodic Content

- The rise of streaming platforms offers opportunities for long-form storytelling, allowing for complex narratives centered on the Golem's origins, evolution, and adventures.
- **Example:** A fantasy mini-series where a baker's descendants uncover the secrets of their ancestor's Gingerbread Golem, unraveling a family legacy intertwined with magical lore.

6. Educational and Inspirational Uses

The Gingerbread Golem's symbolic and narrative richness makes it a valuable tool for education and inspiration in various fields.

6.1 Teaching Tools

- The Golem's myth could be used to teach lessons in ethics, storytelling, and cultural traditions in schools and workshops.
- **Example:** A classroom activity where students create their own Gingerbread Golems while discussing the moral and creative responsibilities of their characters.

6.2 Motivational Symbolism

- The Golem could serve as an inspirational figure, representing resilience, creativity, and the power of community in challenging times.
- **Example:** Community initiatives where Gingerbread Golem imagery is used to foster hope and unity, particularly during holiday seasons.

7. The Golem in Future Rituals and Celebrations

The Gingerbread Golem could become an even more integral part of holiday traditions, evolving alongside societal changes.

7.1 Digital Holiday Celebrations

- Virtual and hybrid celebrations could incorporate Gingerbread Golem crafting into online community events, fostering connection across distances.
- **Example:** A global online competition where participants design and animate digital Gingerbread Golems, celebrating creativity and togetherness.

7.2 New Year's Traditions

- The Golem could take on a symbolic role in New Year's celebrations, representing protection, renewal, and hope for the future.
- **Example:** Communities might create and share Golem-themed desserts as part of a collective wish for prosperity and harmony.

Recurring Themes for the Future

As the Gingerbread Golem myth evolves, certain themes are likely to remain central to its narratives and adaptations:

1. **Creation and Responsibility:**
    - The ethical implications of creation will continue to resonate, especially in discussions of technology and sustainability.
2. **Community and Unity:**
    - The Golem's protective role aligns with contemporary values of collaboration and resilience in the face of challenges.
3. **Transformation and Impermanence:**
    - The Golem's ephemeral nature serves as a reminder of life's cycles and the beauty of renewal.
4. **Imagination and Innovation:**
    - The myth's adaptability ensures its continued relevance in fostering creativity and inspiring new forms of expression.

Conclusion

The Gingerbread Golem's future is as rich and diverse as its storied past. Through digital innovation, cultural reinterpretation, and continued artistic exploration, this enduring figure will remain a symbol of humanity's creativity, resilience, and evolving values. As it bridges the realms of folklore, technology, and culture, the Gingerbread Golem will continue to inspire wonder and connection, proving that even the sweetest myths can have profound and lasting significance.

Chapter 25: The Golem as Archetype

Concluding Reflections on the Gingerbread Golem as an Archetype in Mythology

The Gingerbread Golem occupies a unique and enduring place in the pantheon of mythical constructs. Its story—rooted in themes of creation, protection, impermanence, and morality—resonates across cultures and eras, making it a powerful archetype in mythology. This final chapter explores the Gingerbread Golem's symbolic role as an archetype, reflecting on its significance in folklore, literature, and culture, and considering its broader implications for understanding the human experience.

Defining the Gingerbread Golem Archetype

An archetype is a universal symbol or pattern deeply embedded in the collective human psyche. The Gingerbread Golem, as an archetype, embodies the tension between creation and destruction, the transient nature of existence, and the potential for both good and ill in human endeavors.

Core Characteristics of the Gingerbread Golem Archetype

1. **The Protector:**
    - At its heart, the Gingerbread Golem represents a figure created to safeguard a person, community, or ideal. Its primary function as a defender aligns it with archetypal guardians found in myths worldwide.
2. **The Construct:**
    - Like other mythical constructs, the Gingerbread Golem embodies humanity's desire to create life from nonliving matter, reflecting our need to exercise agency and control over the world.

3. **Ephemeral Nature:**
    - The Golem's impermanence, tied to its edible form, serves as a reminder of life's transience and the inevitability of change and renewal.
4. **The Duality of Creation:**
    - The Gingerbread Golem symbolizes the moral complexity of creation. It can act as a force for good or become a destructive entity, depending on the intentions and actions of its creator.

Mythological Parallels

The Gingerbread Golem shares commonalities with other archetypes in global mythology, situating it within a broader tradition of symbolic figures.

1. The Golem in Jewish Folklore

- The traditional golem, a humanoid figure made of clay and animated through mystical means, serves as a clear precursor to the Gingerbread Golem. Both figures highlight themes of protection, responsibility, and the unintended consequences of creation.

2. Guardian Figures Across Cultures

- The Gingerbread Golem can be compared to other protective archetypes, such as:
    - **The Terracotta Warriors (China):** Constructs created to protect Emperor Qin Shi Huang in the afterlife.
    - **Hearth Spirits (Slavic Folklore):** Protective entities tied to the home and family.
    - **Kachina Spirits (Hopi Mythology):** Figures imbued with spiritual significance, serving as mediators between the divine and human realms.

3. The Archetype of the Ephemeral Hero

- The Gingerbread Golem's inevitable destruction aligns it with heroes whose stories end in self-sacrifice, such as the Greek Prometheus or the Norse Baldur.

Themes and Symbolism in the Gingerbread Golem Archetype
The Gingerbread Golem archetype encapsulates universal themes that resonate across cultural and historical contexts.

1. Creation and Responsibility

- The Golem's existence forces its creator to confront the ethical implications of their actions. Its behavior reflects the creator's intentions, highlighting the idea that power and creativity must be wielded responsibly.
- **Symbolism:**
  - The Golem as a mirror of its creator emphasizes the interconnectedness of action and consequence.

2. Protection and Sacrifice

- As a protector, the Gingerbread Golem often sacrifices itself for the greater good, reinforcing themes of loyalty and altruism.
- **Symbolism:**
  - The Golem's self-sacrifice serves as a metaphor for resilience and the enduring impact of transient acts of courage and kindness.

3. Impermanence and Transformation

- The Golem's edible form underscores its temporary nature, reflecting the cycles of life, death, and renewal.
- **Symbolism:**

- The inevitability of the Golem's destruction mirrors the human condition, encouraging acceptance of change and loss.

4. Duality and Ambiguity

- The Gingerbread Golem's potential for both benevolence and malevolence reflects the dual nature of creation and the complexity of human intentions.
- **Symbolism:**
  - The Golem as a moral lesson reminds us that even well-meaning creations can have unintended consequences.

The Gingerbread Golem's Role in Modern Culture

In contemporary contexts, the Gingerbread Golem archetype continues to evolve, adapting to new cultural narratives and challenges.

1. A Symbol of Creativity and Innovation

- The Golem represents the human drive to create and innovate, serving as an inspiration for artists, writers, and thinkers.

2. A Metaphor for Ethical Challenges

- The archetype's emphasis on responsibility and consequences makes it a fitting metaphor for modern issues, such as technological advancements, environmental stewardship, and social justice.

3. A Beacon of Hope and Resilience

- As a protector and symbol of self-sacrifice, the Golem inspires hope and unity, particularly in times of hardship or uncertainty.

The Gingerbread Golem and the Collective Human Experience

The Gingerbread Golem's enduring appeal lies in its ability to embody fundamental aspects of the human experience:

1. **The Desire to Protect:**
    - The Golem's role as a guardian speaks to humanity's innate need to create safety and stability in a chaotic world.
2. **The Act of Creation:**
    - The Golem's construction symbolizes the human drive to shape and transform the environment, imbuing it with meaning and purpose.
3. **The Acceptance of Impermanence:**
    - The Golem's ephemeral nature encourages reflection on the transient beauty of life and the importance of cherishing the present.
4. **The Search for Meaning:**
    - As both a mystical creation and a moral lesson, the Golem invites contemplation of the deeper questions of existence, purpose, and legacy.

Conclusion: The Gingerbread Golem as a Timeless Archetype

The Gingerbread Golem transcends its origins as a festive creation to become a universal archetype, embodying themes of protection, creativity, and morality that resonate across time and cultures. Its adaptability ensures its continued relevance, allowing it to inspire new interpretations and innovations while remaining rooted in its mythological foundations. As a symbol of humanity's aspirations, struggles, and triumphs, the Gingerbread Golem reminds us of the enduring power of stories to illuminate our shared journey and guide us toward a sweeter future.

Appendices

Appendix A: Recipe Compendium

Historical and Mythical Recipes for Creating Gingerbread Golems, Including Variations

This appendix presents a detailed collection of historical and mythical recipes for crafting Gingerbread Golems, blending culinary tradition with folkloric magic. From traditional European methods to modern adaptations, these recipes offer insight into the symbolic and practical elements of Gingerbread Golem creation. Each recipe includes ingredients, techniques, and variations tailored for specific purposes or cultural contexts.

1. The Classic Protector's Recipe

A Traditional Bavarian Recipe for a Guardian Golem

This recipe, originating in 16th-century Bavaria, was often used to craft Golems during winter festivals. It emphasizes strength and longevity.

Ingredients:

- 4 cups all-purpose flour (symbolizing stability and grounding)
- 1 cup unsalted butter, softened (representing unity and cohesion)
- 1 cup molasses (symbolizing warmth and abundance)
- 3/4 cup dark brown sugar
- 2 tablespoons ground ginger (the "heart" of the Golem)
- 1 tablespoon cinnamon (protection)
- 1 teaspoon ground cloves (endurance)
- 1 teaspoon nutmeg (intuition)
- 1 teaspoon baking soda
- 1/4 teaspoon salt (purity and protection)
- 1 egg (symbolizing life)

Instructions:

1. Preparation of Dough:
    - In a large mixing bowl, cream butter, sugar, and molasses until smooth.
    - Add the egg and mix until incorporated.
    - Sift together dry ingredients (flour, spices, baking soda, and salt) and gradually mix into the wet ingredients until a firm dough forms.
    - Chill the dough for at least 2 hours to ensure stability.
2. Shaping the Golem:
    - Roll out the dough on a floured surface to 1/4-inch thickness.
    - Cut out Golem shapes using hand-crafted wooden molds or freehand with a knife. Ensure the figure has robust limbs and a defined heart area for decoration.
3. Decoration:
    - Use icing to draw protective symbols (e.g., spirals, stars, or runes) on the Golem's body.
    - Add candy eyes for vigilance and a red candy heart to symbolize vitality.
4. Baking:
    - Bake at 350°F (175°C) for 12-15 minutes or until edges are firm.
5. Activation Ritual (Optional):
    - Place the baked Golem in a circle of candles and recite a protective chant to "animate" its symbolic qualities.

2. The Frost Guardian's Recipe

A Scandinavian Variation for Winter Protection

This version incorporates cooling flavors and icy decorations to emphasize the Golem's role as a winter guardian.

Ingredients:

- 3 1/2 cups rye flour (reflecting Nordic agricultural traditions)
- 1 cup honey (for warmth and community)
- 1/2 cup unsalted butter
- 3/4 cup white sugar
- 1 teaspoon ground cardamom (spiritual clarity)
- 1 tablespoon ground ginger
- 1 teaspoon anise seeds (protection against spirits)
- 1/2 teaspoon salt
- 2 egg whites (for snow-like frosting)

Instructions:

1. Preparation:
    - Heat honey and butter in a saucepan until melted. Let cool slightly, then mix with sugar.
    - Combine dry ingredients in a bowl and gradually add to the honey mixture to form a dough. Chill for 2 hours.
2. Shaping and Design:
    - Roll out the dough to 1/3-inch thickness and cut into Golem shapes.
    - Create frost-like patterns using royal icing made from whipped egg whites and powdered sugar.
3. Baking:
    - Bake at 325°F (160°C) for 15 minutes or until golden brown.

4. Optional Activation:
    - Use a small silver bell to "wake" the Golem and invite it to guard during the winter months.

3. The Sweet Avenger's Recipe
A French-Inspired Recipe for Heroic Golems

This luxurious recipe includes almond flour and spices, emphasizing elegance and strength.

Ingredients:

- 2 cups almond flour (symbolizing strength and resilience)
- 2 cups all-purpose flour
- 1 cup powdered sugar
- 1 cup unsalted butter, softened
- 1/4 cup orange blossom honey (representing bravery)
- 2 teaspoons cinnamon
- 1 teaspoon ginger
- 1 teaspoon vanilla extract (purity and intent)
- 1 egg yolk (to bind the Golem's spirit)

Instructions:

1. Preparation:
    - Combine almond flour, all-purpose flour, powdered sugar, and spices.
    - Mix in butter, honey, and vanilla extract until dough forms. Chill for 1 hour.
2. Shaping:
    - Sculpt heroic poses for the Golem, such as an arm raised in defense. Add decorative details like shields or armor with icing.
3. Baking and Decoration:
    - Bake at 350°F (175°C) for 10-12 minutes. Once cooled, paint gold accents using edible gold dust mixed with vodka or lemon extract.
4. Optional Blessing:

- Sprinkle the Golem with powdered sugar while reciting words of courage and protection.

4. The Woodland Golem Recipe

An Eco-Friendly Recipe for Nature Guardians

Designed for sustainability, this recipe uses plant-based ingredients and earthy decorations.

Ingredients:

- 2 1/2 cups whole wheat flour (representing the earth)
- 1/2 cup coconut oil (renewable resource)
- 1/2 cup maple syrup (symbolizing the forest's bounty)
- 1/2 cup almond milk
- 1 tablespoon ground flaxseed (binding agent)
- 1 teaspoon cinnamon
- 1 teaspoon ginger
- 1/2 teaspoon nutmeg
- Dried fruit and seeds for decoration

Instructions:

1. Preparation:
    - Mix coconut oil, maple syrup, and almond milk until smooth.
    - Combine dry ingredients in a separate bowl, then mix into the wet ingredients to form a dough. Chill for 1 hour.
2. Shaping:

- Roll out the dough and cut Golem shapes with wide, tree-like limbs. Decorate with dried fruit for eyes and seeds for protective patterns.
3. Baking:
    - Bake at 325°F (160°C) for 15 minutes or until lightly browned.
4. Ritual Placement:
    - Place the Golem outdoors as a symbolic protector of natural spaces.

5. The Festive Golem Recipe

A Modern Recipe for Celebratory Occasions

This fun and accessible recipe is designed for family crafting during holidays.

Ingredients:

- 4 cups all-purpose flour
- 1 cup brown sugar
- 1 cup unsalted butter, softened
- 1/2 cup molasses
- 2 teaspoons baking soda
- 1 tablespoon ginger
- 2 teaspoons cinnamon
- 1 teaspoon allspice
- Candy, icing, and edible glitter for decoration

Instructions:

1. Preparation:
    - Cream butter, sugar, and molasses. Mix dry ingredients separately, then combine with wet ingredients to form a dough. Chill for 1 hour.
2. Shaping and Decoration:
    - Cut festive Golem shapes and let children decorate with colorful icing, candies, and glitter.
3. Baking:
    - Bake at 350°F (175°C) for 12-15 minutes.
4. Family Ritual:
    - Gather around the Golem, share a wish, and enjoy it as part of the holiday feast.

Conclusion

These recipes reflect the rich diversity of Gingerbread Golem traditions, blending culinary expertise with symbolic significance. Whether created for protection, celebration, or connection to nature, each Golem carries a unique story, making the process of baking and decorating an act of creativity and intention. By crafting these Golems, modern bakers honor a timeless myth while adding their own personal touch to the sweet legacy.

Appendix B: Annotated Folktales

Full Transcriptions and Annotations of Major Gingerbread Golem Stories from Around the World

This appendix provides full transcriptions and detailed annotations of key Gingerbread Golem folktales from various cultures. Each tale is accompanied by commentary on its themes, symbolism, and historical significance, offering insights into the diverse interpretations and cultural roles of the Gingerbread Golem myth.

1. The Guardian of Spicedown

Origin: German Folklore (16th Century)

Story Transcription:

In a small Bavarian village called Spicedown, the winters were long and unforgiving. One year, as snow fell endlessly and wolves prowled near the village, the baker Hans devised a plan to protect his home and neighbors. Using the finest flour, honey, and spices from his pantry, Hans baked a life-sized figure of gingerbread, shaping it into a sturdy protector with broad shoulders and watchful eyes made of sugar pearls.

As the Golem baked in the oven, Hans whispered a blessing:
"With warmth from the hearth, may you guard this place. With sweetness in your heart, may you keep us safe."

When the Golem emerged from the oven, it stood upright, its sugar eyes glowing faintly in the candlelight. For weeks, it patrolled the village, warding off wolves and keeping thieves at bay. But as winter thawed into spring, the Golem began to crumble, its task complete. The villagers gathered its remains and buried them under the oldest tree in the village, planting ginger root nearby to honor their protector.

Annotations:

- **Themes:**
  - Protection and Sacrifice: The Golem's creation reflects the communal need for safety and the willingness to sacrifice even temporary creations for the greater good.
  - Impermanence: The Golem's gradual crumbling mirrors the natural cycles of life and renewal.
- **Symbolism:**
  - Ingredients: The use of ginger and honey represents warmth and community, essential for survival during harsh winters.
  - Burial and Ginger Plant: The planting of ginger root ties the Golem's essence to the land, ensuring its protective spirit endures.
- **Cultural Context:**
  - This tale highlights the importance of resourcefulness and collaboration during difficult times, reflecting the harsh realities of rural life in 16th-century Bavaria.

2. The Frosted Sentinel

Origin: Scandinavian Folklore (18th Century)

Story Transcription:

In the frozen north, the village of Snøland faced an endless blizzard one Yule season. Fearing the wrath of the Frost King, the villagers gathered in the longhouse to devise a plan. An elderly baker, Ingrid, suggested crafting a Gingerbread Golem to shield the village from the icy winds.

Using her family's ancient recipe, Ingrid baked a giant Golem, adding a pinch of salt from the fjord and sprinkling its body with silver sugar dust to reflect the frost. She recited the sacred chant passed down through generations:

"From dough and spice, strong and true,
Stand and guard, protect our due."

The Golem rose, its frosting shimmering like snow under the moonlight. For twelve nights, it stood at the village's edge, holding back the Frost King's wrath. On the thirteenth night, as the blizzard ended, the Golem cracked and dissolved into the snow, its task fulfilled. In its place, the villagers found a single gingerbread tree, its leaves perpetually sweet and fragrant.

Annotations:

- **Themes:**
    - Resilience: The Golem symbolizes the strength needed to endure harsh conditions.
    - Harmony with Nature: The transformation of the Golem into a tree represents renewal and balance with the environment.
- **Symbolism:**

- Silver Sugar Dust: A protective charm, reflecting the light of the moon and serving as a shield against cold and darkness.
- Thirteen Nights: A reference to the Yule season, emphasizing the Golem's connection to winter rituals.
- **Cultural Context:**
  - This tale reflects the Nordic reverence for nature and seasonal cycles, blending the magical and the practical.

3. The Sweet Avenger
Origin: French Folklore (17th Century)
Story Transcription:

In the bustling city of Bordeaux, a greedy nobleman, Count Gaston, taxed the peasants heavily, leaving them hungry and desperate. In secret, the village baker Claudette baked a Gingerbread Golem, using the spices she had hidden from the count's guards. She adorned the Golem with almond slices for armor and a candy cane staff as its weapon.

On a moonlit night, Claudette brought the Golem to life with a whisper:

"By sweet and spice, justice be done.
Stand tall and fight until the battle is won."

The Golem stormed the count's manor, scattering his guards and retrieving stolen grain for the villagers. Over the following nights, it patrolled the streets, ensuring fairness and peace. Once the nobleman fled, the Golem climbed to the cathedral's bell tower and crumbled into sugar dust, which the villagers collected to sweeten their bread for years to come.

Annotations:

- **Themes:**
    - Justice and Empowerment: The Golem acts as an agent of justice, reflecting the villagers' desire for fairness.
    - Legacy: The sugar dust symbolizes the lasting impact of the Golem's actions.
- **Symbolism:**
    - Almond Armor: A nod to strength and protection, using locally available materials.
    - Candy Cane Staff: A playful yet potent symbol of power and sweetness.
- **Cultural Context:**

- This tale reflects the tensions between peasants and nobility in pre-revolutionary France, using the Golem as a symbol of rebellion and justice.

4. The Mischievous Golem

Origin: English Folklore (19th Century)

Story Transcription:

In a small English village, the baker Edward crafted a Gingerbread Golem each Christmas to protect the children's gifts from mischievous sprites. One year, Edward's apprentice, Tommy, decided to experiment with the recipe, adding too much cinnamon and leaving the dough unfinished.

When the Golem rose, it was smaller and nimbler than usual, with mischievous eyes and a tendency to play pranks. Instead of guarding the gifts, it hid them around the village, leading the children on a wild treasure hunt. The villagers, amused by the Golem's antics, forgave its mischief. After the holiday, the Golem crumbled into crumbs, which were baked into cookies for the next year's feast.

Annotations:

- **Themes:**
    - Playfulness: The Golem's mischief emphasizes the joy and spontaneity of the holiday season.
    - Redemption: The Golem's crumbs are transformed into cookies, symbolizing forgiveness and renewal.
- **Symbolism:**
    - Cinnamon Overload: A metaphor for imperfection, showing that even flaws can lead to joy.
    - Hidden Gifts: Reflecting the spirit of discovery and the value of community participation.
- **Cultural Context:**
    - This lighthearted tale mirrors Victorian England's emphasis on family and festive traditions during Christmas.

Conclusion

These folktales illustrate the versatility and richness of the Gingerbread Golem archetype, adapting its themes to different cultural and historical contexts. From fierce protectors to playful mischief-makers, the Golem embodies universal values of resilience, justice, and community. Through these annotated stories, the enduring legacy of the Gingerbread Golem is preserved, offering timeless lessons and inspiration for generations to come.

Appendix C: Symbols and Ingredients

In-Depth Analysis of Symbols and Their Meanings in the Myths

The Gingerbread Golem myths are rich with symbolic elements, with each ingredient, decoration, and ritual gesture carrying layers of meaning. This appendix explores these symbols and their significance, highlighting how they contribute to the Golem's mythos as a protector, creation, and symbol of human creativity and morality.

1. Key Ingredients and Their Symbolism

The ingredients used to create a Gingerbread Golem are not merely culinary but are imbued with metaphorical meanings that align with the myth's themes of protection, resilience, and impermanence.

1.1 Flour

- **Symbolism:** Stability, grounding, and the foundation of creation.
- **Context:** Flour represents the earth, anchoring the Golem to the physical world. Its use reflects humanity's connection to nature and the material.

1.2 Ginger

- **Symbolism:** Warmth, vitality, and the "heart" of the Golem.
- **Context:** Ginger is a spice historically associated with protection and healing. Its inclusion symbolizes the life force animating the Golem and its role as a guardian.

1.3 Molasses or Honey

- **Symbolism:** Abundance, unity, and the sweetness of community.
- **Context:** These ingredients bind the dough together, metaphorically uniting the community or the creator's intentions. They also reflect themes of generosity and shared resources.

1.4 Spices (Cinnamon, Clove, Nutmeg, Cardamom)

- **Symbolism:** Protection, spiritual clarity, and inner strength.
- **Context:** Each spice carries its own significance:
    - **Cinnamon:** A purifier that protects against negative forces.
    - **Clove:** Endurance and persistence in the face of adversity.
    - **Nutmeg:** Intuition and hidden wisdom.
    - **Cardamom:** Connection to higher spiritual realms.

1.5 Salt

- **Symbolism:** Purity, protection, and preservation.
- **Context:** Salt is often used in rituals to ward off evil spirits. In the Golem, it acts as a metaphysical safeguard, preventing corruption of its purpose.

1.6 Eggs

- **Symbolism:** Life, creation, and the spark of animation.
- **Context:** Eggs represent the potential for life and transformation, aligning with the Golem's role as a creation brought to life.

1.7 Sugar

- **Symbolism:** Energy, sweetness, and celebration.
- **Context:** Sugar not only enhances the Golem's festive appearance but also symbolizes the joy and hope it brings to its community.

2. Decorations and Their Symbolism

The decorative elements of the Gingerbread Golem are imbued with protective and aesthetic significance, reinforcing its role as a guardian and cultural icon.

2.1 Candy Eyes

- **Symbolism:** Vigilance and awareness.
- **Context:** The eyes, often made of sugar pearls or candies, symbolize the Golem's ability to watch over and protect its creator or community.

2.2 Red Candy Heart

- **Symbolism:** Vitality, compassion, and the essence of life.
- **Context:** The heart is frequently marked with a red candy or icing, serving as a focal point for the Golem's animation rituals and representing its life force.

2.3 Icing Patterns (Runes and Symbols)

- **Symbolism:** Magical protection and intention.
- **Context:** Protective symbols such as spirals, stars, or sigils are drawn with icing to imbue the Golem with its purpose. Common patterns include:
  - **Circles:** Unity and eternal protection.
  - **Stars:** Guidance and divine favor.
  - **Spirals:** Growth and resilience.

2.4 Gold or Silver Dust

- **Symbolism:** Divine energy and strength.
- **Context:** Metallic decorations enhance the Golem's appearance while symbolizing its elevated role as a magical protector.

2.5 Candy Buttons and Accessories

- **Symbolism:** Individuality and charm.
- **Context:** These details personalize the Golem, reinforcing its connection to its creator and community.

3. Ritual Elements in Animation

The process of animating a Gingerbread Golem involves symbolic gestures and chants that align with its purpose, enhancing its mystical significance.

3.1 Chanting and Incantations

- **Symbolism:** The power of words and intention.
- **Context:** Chants used in the animation process often include elements of gratitude, protection, and purpose, reflecting the creator's desires.

3.2 Tracing Symbols

- **Symbolism:** Directing energy and focus.
- **Context:** Tracing protective symbols or runes over the Golem with a finger or tool channels energy into specific aspects of its role, such as guarding a home or community.

3.3 Lighting Candles

- **Symbolism:** Awakening and illumination.
- **Context:** Candles placed around the Golem during its animation ritual symbolize the spark of life and the light it brings to its surroundings.

4. Mythical Variations in Symbolism

Different cultures and regions have adapted the Gingerbread Golem myth to reflect their unique traditions and beliefs, resulting in variations in its symbols and ingredients.

4.1 Nordic Frost Guardian

- **Ingredients:** Incorporates salt from the fjords and cardamom for clarity.
- **Decorations:** Frost-like patterns with silver sugar dust to reflect winter themes.
- **Symbolism:** The Golem's shimmering appearance represents its harmony with the snowy landscape, emphasizing protection against harsh elements.

4.2 French Sweet Avenger

- **Ingredients:** Almond flour and orange blossom honey, symbolizing resilience and bravery.
- **Decorations:** Gold accents and candy cane weapons reflect its role as a justice-bringer.
- **Symbolism:** This version of the Golem emphasizes empowerment and fairness, addressing themes of social inequality.

4.3 Woodland Protector

- **Ingredients:** Whole wheat flour and seeds, representing nature's abundance.
- **Decorations:** Natural embellishments like dried fruit and edible flowers.
- **Symbolism:** The Golem's rustic appearance connects it to the earth, reinforcing its role as a guardian of the natural world.

5. Broader Symbolic Themes

The ingredients and decorations of the Gingerbread Golem carry broader symbolic meanings that resonate universally.

5.1 Creation and Intention

- The Golem's composition reflects the care and intention of its creator, emphasizing the interconnectedness of human actions and their outcomes.

5.2 Community and Unity

- Many elements, such as shared ingredients or communal baking rituals, highlight the Golem's role as a symbol of collective effort and solidarity.

5.3 Transience and Legacy

- The edible nature of the Golem underscores the impermanence of its form, while its symbolic impact endures through its actions and the memories it inspires.

5.4 Duality of Power

- The Golem's potential for both protection and destruction reflects the moral complexities of creation, reminding us of the responsibility inherent in wielding power.

Conclusion

The symbols and ingredients associated with the Gingerbread Golem myth deepen its cultural and narrative significance, transforming it from a simple festive figure into a profound archetype. By understanding these elements, we gain insight into the values, fears, and aspirations of the communities that created and sustained this enduring legend. Through its rich symbolism, the Gingerbread Golem continues to inspire stories, traditions, and creativity across generations.

Appendix D: Chronology of Gingerbread Golem Legends

Timeline of the Evolution of the Gingerbread Golem Across History and Cultures

The Gingerbread Golem's journey from a humble figure of folklore to a celebrated symbol in global culture is marked by centuries of evolution. This appendix provides a detailed timeline of the key historical and cultural developments that shaped the myth, highlighting its transformations, adaptations, and enduring appeal.

1. Early Foundations (Pre-14th Century)

Proto-Golem Myths and Culinary Traditions

- **2000 BCE - 500 BCE: The Dawn of Construct Myths**
    - Early myths in Mesopotamia and Egypt feature constructs such as clay figures animated by gods or priests, laying the conceptual groundwork for later Golem legends.
    - Culinary effigies, like ritual bread figures in ancient Egypt, are crafted for religious purposes, symbolizing protection, fertility, or offerings to deities.
- **1st Century CE: Roman Honey Cakes and Edible Guardians**
    - The Romans craft edible figures made from honey and flour, called *libum*, for festivals. These may have inspired later traditions of baking protective figures during seasonal rituals.

2. The Medieval Period (10th–15th Century)
Emergence of Golem Myths and the Rise of Gingerbread

- **10th Century: Jewish Golem Stories in Eastern Europe**
    - The Golem legend emerges in Jewish mysticism, featuring clay figures brought to life by sacred incantations. These stories introduce themes of protection, impermanence, and creator responsibility.
    - The concept of a protective construct influences other cultural myths, including edible effigies.
- **13th Century: Gingerbread Introduced to Europe**
    - Crusaders bring ginger and other spices back from the Middle East, leading to the rise of gingerbread in European cuisine.
    - Gingerbread figures become popular in monasteries, where they are crafted for religious festivals and as symbols of protection.
- **14th Century: Proto-Gingerbread Golem Tales**
    - Early mentions of edible protectors appear in Germanic and Scandinavian folklore, describing bread or cake figures baked to ward off evil during harsh winters.

3. The Renaissance and Early Modern Era (16th–18th Century)
Formalization of Gingerbread Golem Legends

- **1520–1550: The Guardian of Spicedown**
    - One of the earliest documented Gingerbread Golem stories emerges in Bavaria, detailing a life-sized gingerbread figure crafted to protect a village from wolves.
    - The tale reflects the increasing association of gingerbread with protective and festive roles.
- **1600s: Gingerbread in Holiday Traditions**
    - Gingerbread effigies become central to Christmas and Yule celebrations across Europe, blending culinary artistry with protective symbolism.
    - Stories of Gingerbread Golems as seasonal guardians proliferate in regions such as Germany, Austria, and Scandinavia.
- **1693: French Tale "The Sweet Avenger"**
    - In Bordeaux, the Gingerbread Golem is reimagined as a justice-bringer, retrieving stolen goods from a corrupt nobleman.
    - This marks a shift from purely protective roles to narratives emphasizing moral and social justice.

4. The Enlightenment and Romantic Eras (18th–19th Century)
Expansion of the Myth into Literature and Art

- **1740s: Gingerbread Golem Operettas in Germany and Austria**
    - Early theatrical adaptations of the Gingerbread Golem myth appear in operettas, blending folklore with music and performance.
- **1790–1810: Folklore Documentation**
    - German and French folklorists, such as Johann Fischer and Émile Renaud, begin documenting Gingerbread Golem tales, preserving oral traditions.
    - These collections establish the Golem as a recurring figure in European folklore.
- **19th Century: Victorian Christmas Traditions**
    - In England, Gingerbread Golems gain popularity as part of Victorian Christmas celebrations.
    - Tales such as *"The Mischievous Golem"* introduce a playful element to the myth, reflecting the era's emphasis on family and festivity.

5. The Modern Era (20th–21st Century)
Global Adaptation and Cultural Expansion

- **1920s–1930s: Gingerbread Golems in Children's Literature**
    - The Golem becomes a beloved figure in children's books, such as *"Ginger the Brave,"* where it takes on adventurous and whimsical roles.
- **1950s: Golden Age of Gingerbread Golem Musicals**
    - Broadway and regional theaters stage musicals featuring Gingerbread Golem characters, often emphasizing themes of courage, community, and festive joy.
- **1980s–1990s: Fantasy and Speculative Fiction**
    - Fantasy novels and role-playing games reimagine the Gingerbread Golem as a magical construct with unique abilities, expanding its myth into new genres.
- **2000s: Digital Media and Animation**
    - Animated films and digital art platforms bring the Gingerbread Golem to global audiences, with adaptations that blend traditional narratives with contemporary themes.
- **2020s: Eco-Conscious Interpretations**
    - The Golem is reimagined in stories and art as a symbol of environmental stewardship, emphasizing sustainable creation and harmony with nature.

6. Cross-Cultural Variations and Global Impact

The Gingerbread Golem has transcended its European roots, blending with local myths and traditions around the world.

Asia (21st Century):

- Japanese artists reinterpret the Golem in *kawaii* (cute) aesthetics, featuring pastel colors and playful designs in manga and anime.

North America (20th–21st Century):

- The Golem becomes a fixture in holiday marketing, films, and theme park attractions, representing joy and festivity.
- Indigenous artists incorporate the Golem into narratives emphasizing protection of natural resources.

Africa (21st Century):

- African storytellers blend the Gingerbread Golem with guardian spirits, emphasizing its role in protecting crops and communities.

7. Key Themes in the Chronology
Creation and Responsibility:

- From its early roots in Jewish mysticism to modern environmental interpretations, the Golem consistently reflects humanity's ethical dilemmas in creating and controlling life.

Protection and Community:

- The Gingerbread Golem's role as a guardian of homes, villages, and values has remained central throughout its evolution.

Festivity and Creativity:

- As a symbol of celebration, the Golem bridges the realms of culinary art and folklore, inspiring joy and creativity across generations.

Impermanence and Renewal:

- The Golem's edible nature underscores its transient existence, reminding audiences of the cycles of life, death, and rebirth.

Conclusion

The Gingerbread Golem's journey across centuries and cultures reflects its adaptability and universal appeal. From its early roots as a protector in folklore to its modern reinterpretations in digital media and global storytelling, the Golem continues to evolve, embodying the themes of creation, community, and resilience that resonate deeply with humanity. This chronology highlights the enduring relevance of the Gingerbread Golem as both a mythological archetype and a cultural icon.

Message from the Author:

I hope you enjoyed this book, I love astrology and knew there was not a book such as this out on the shelf. I love metaphysical items as well. Please check out my other books:

-Life of Government Benefits

-My life of Hell

-My life with Hydrocephalus

-Red Sky

-World Domination:Woman's rule

-World Domination:Woman's Rule 2: The War

-Life and Banishment of Apophis: book 1

-The Kidney Friendly Diet

-The Ultimate Hemp Cookbook

-Creating a Dispensary(legally)

-Cleanliness throughout life: the importance of showering from childhood to adulthood.

-Strong Roots: The Risks of Overcoddling children

-Hemp Horoscopes: Cosmic Insights and Earthly Healing

- Celestial Hemp Navigating the Zodiac: Through the Green Cosmos

-Astrological Hemp: Aligning The Stars with Earth's Ancient Herb

-The Astrological Guide to Hemp: Stars, Signs, and Sacred Leaves

-Green Growth: Innovative Marketing Strategies for your Hemp Products and Dispensary

-Cosmic Cannabis

-Astrological Munchies

-Henry The Hemp

-Zodiacal Roots: The Astrological Soul Of Hemp

- **Green Constellations: Intersection of Hemp and Zodiac**

-Hemp in The Houses: An astrological Adventure Through The Cannabis Galaxy

-Galactic Ganja Guide

Heavenly Hemp
Zodiac Leaves
Doctor Who Astrology
Cannastrology
Stellar Satvias and Cosmic Indicas
<u>Celestial Cannabis: A Zodiac Journey</u>
AstroHerbology: The Sky and The Soil: Volume 1
AstroHerbology:Celestial Cannabis:Volume 2
Cosmic Cannabis Cultivation
The Starry Guide to Herbal Harmony: Volume 1
The Starry Guide to Herbal Harmony: Cannabis Universe: Volume 2

Yugioh Astrology: Astrological Guide to Deck, Duels and more
Nightmare Mansion: Echoes of The Abyss
Nightmare Mansion 2: Legacy of Shadows
Nightmare Mansion 3: Shadows of the Forgotten
Nightmare Mansion 4: Echoes of the Damned
The Life and Banishment of Apophis: Book 2
Nightmare Mansion: Halls of Despair
<u>Healing with Herb: Cannabis and Hydrocephalus</u>
Planetary Pot: Aligning with Astrological Herbs: Volume 1
Fast Track to Freedom: 30 Days to Financial Independence Using AI, Assets, and Agile Hustles
<u>Cosmic Hemp Pathways</u>
How to Become Financially Free in 30 Days: 10,000 Paths to Prosperity
Zodiacal Herbage: Astrological Insights: Volume 1
Nightmare Mansion: Whispers in the Walls
The Daleks Invade Atlantis
Henry the hemp and Hydrocephalus

10X The Kidney Friendly Diet
Cannabis Universe: Adult coloring book

Hemp Astrology: The Healing Power of the Stars
Zodiacal Herbage: Astrological Insights: Cannabis Universe: Volume 2
Planetary Pot: Aligning with Astrological Herbs: Cannabis Universes: Volume 2
Doctor Who Meets the Replicators and SG-1: The Ultimate Battle for Survival
Nightmare Mansion: Curse of the Blood Moon
The Celestial Stoner: A Guide to the Zodiac
Cosmic Pleasures: Sex Toy Astrology for Every Sign
Hydrocephalus Astrology: Navigating the Stars and Healing Waters
Lapis and the Mischievous Chocolate Bar

Celestial Positions: Sexual Astrology for Every Sign
Apophis's Shadow Work Journal: : A Journey of Self-Discovery and Healing
Kinky Cosmos: Sexual Kink Astrology for Every Sign
Digital Cosmos: The Astrological Digimon Compendium
Stellar Seeds: The Cosmic Guide to Growing with Astrology
Apophis's Daily Gratitude Journal

Cat Astrology: Feline Mysteries of the Cosmos
The Cosmic Kama Sutra: An Astrological Guide to Sexual Positions
Unleash Your Potential: A Guided Journal Powered by AI Insights
Whispers of the Enchanted Grove

Cosmic Pleasures: An Astrological Guide to Sexual Kinks
369, 12 Manifestation Journal
Whisper of the nocturne journal(blank journal for writing or drawing)

The Boogey Book
Locked In Reflection: A Chastity Journey Through Locktober
Generating Wealth Quickly:
How to Generate $100,000 in 24 Hours
Star Magic: Harness the Power of the Universe
The Flatulence Chronicles: A Fart Journal for Self-Discovery
The Doctor and The Death Moth
Seize the Day: A Personal Seizure Tracking Journal
The Ultimate Boogeyman Safari: A Journey into the Boogie World and Beyond

Whispers of Samhain: 1,000 Spells of Love, Luck, and Lunar Magic: Samhain Spell Book

Apophis's guides:

Witch's Spellbook Crafting Guide for Halloween

Frost & Flame: The Enchanted Yule Grimoire of 1000 Winter Spells

The Ultimate Boogey Goo Guide & Spooky Activities for Halloween Fun

Harmony of the Scales: A Libra's Spellcraft for Balance and Beauty
The Enchanted Advent: 36 Days of Christmas Wonders

Nightmare Mansion: The Labyrinth of Screams

Harvest of Enchantment: 1,000 Spells of Gratitude, Love, and Fortune for Thanksgiving

The Boogey Chronicles: A Journal of Nightly Encounters and Shadowy Secrets

The 12 Days of Financial Freedom: A Step-by-Step Christmas Countdown to Transform Your Finances

Sigil of the Eternal Spiral Blank Journal

A Christmas Feast: Timeless Recipes for Every Meal

Holiday Stress-Free Solutions: A Survival Guide to Thriving During the Festive Season

Yu-Gi-Oh! Holiday Gifting Mastery: The Ultimate Guide for Fans and Newcomers Alike

Holiday Harmony: A Hydrocephalus Survival Guide for the Festive Season

Celestial Craft: The Witch's Almanac for 2025 – A Cosmic Guide to Manifestations, Moons, and Mystical Events

Doctor Who: The Toymaker's Winter Wonderland

Tulsa King Unveiled: A Thrilling Guide to Stallone's Mafia Masterpiece

Pendulum Craft: A Complete Guide to Crafting and Using Personalized Divination Tools

Nightmare Mansion: Santa's Eternal Eve

Starlight Noel: A Cosmic Journey through Christmas Mysteries

The Dark Architect: Unlocking the Blueprint of Existence

Surviving the Embrace: The Ultimate Guide to Encounters with The Hugging Molly

The Enchanted Codex: Secrets of the Craft for Witches, Wiccans, and Pagans

Harvest of Gratitude: A Complete Thanksgiving Guide

Yuletide Essentials: A Complete Guide to an Authentic and Magical Christmas

Celestial Smokes: A Cosmic Guide to Cigars and Astrology

Living in Balance: A Comprehensive Survival Guide to Thriving with Diabetes Insipidus

Cosmic Symbiosis: The Venom Zodiac Chronicles

The Cursed Paw of Ambition

Cosmic Symbiosis: The Astrological Venom Journal

Celestial Wonders Unfold: A Stargazer's Guide to the Cosmos (2024-2029)

The Ultimate Black Friday Prepper's Guide: Mastering Shopping Strategies and Savings

Cosmic Sales: The Astrological Guide to Black Friday Shopping

Legends of the Corn Mother and Other Harvest Myths

Whispers of the Harvest: The Corn Mother's Journal
The Evergreen Spellbook
The Doctor Meets the Boogeyman
The White Witch of Rose Hall's SpellBook
The Gingerbread Golem's Shadow: A Study in Sweet Darkness
If you want solar for your home go here: https://www.harborsolar.live/apophisenterprises/

Get Some Tarot cards: https://www.makeplayingcards.com/sell/apophis-occult-shop

Get some shirts: https://www.bonfire.com/store/apophis-shirt-emporium/

Instagrams:
@apophis_enterprises,
@apophisbookemporium,
@apophisscardshop
Twitter: @apophisenterpr1
 Tiktok:@apophisenterprise
Youtube: @sg1fan23477, @FiresideRetreatKingdom
Hive: @sg1fan23477
CheeLee: @SG1fan23477

Podcast: Apophis Chat Zone: https://open.spotify.com/show/5zXbrCLEV2xzCp8ybrfHsk?si=fb4d4fdbdce44dec

Newsletter: https://apophiss-newsletter-27c897.beehiiv.com/

Milton Keynes UK
Ingram Content Group UK Ltd.
UKHW021122031224
452078UK00011B/984